In Mondo's compelling book, *My Crazy Life: The Moments That Brought a Gangster to Grace,* he unfolds a riveting tale of transformation. From a life tarnished by crime and violence to daringly escaping one of Los Angeles' most notorious gangs, Mondo's journey is nothing short of extraordinary. Mondo's ability to infuse humor into the darkest moments of his past is a testament to the strength of his character and the grace that now defines his life. This page-turner made Lori and me laugh, it made us cry, and we found ourselves reluctant to put it down. Mondo's story is a tapestry of resilience, redemption, and the enduring grace that can emerge from even the darkest corners of life. Mondo has been loyal and faithful to work by our side for the past twenty-five years. Lori and I have watched him mature into the person he has become today. Not only did Mondo become a friend, but he has become a son to Lori and me. Today, Mondo is the cohost of my television ministry. We know you will enjoy reading his life story. It is a true-life adventure of how a gangster finds Christ and is transformed by God's love.

—JIM AND LORI BAKKER
HOSTS, *THE JIM BAKKER SHOW*

Mary and I are excited to recommend this book by our friend Mondo De La Vega. He has a powerful testimony of coming from a very dysfunctional and broken life. He exemplifies the mercy and grace and power of God offered to everyone to transform and give hope to all who would be willing to submit their lives to the Lord. This is a must-read for anyone who has a child in rebellion, who has no hope, as this book gives encouragement and hope to the hopeless. This book is a powerful tool for any loved ones to come to know Jesus and His transformative power as Savior and Lord of their lives.

—DON COLBERT, MD, AND MARY COLBERT
.ING AUTHORS

T0003634

My Crazy Life is unlike any story I've ever read. I have personally known Mondo for years and have been impacted by his kindness and compassion, which are so apparent even in his eyes. But after reading Mondo's full testimony, I more deeply appreciate him and his totally remarkable story. This is the account of a man whose gangster life has been absolutely revolutionized by the love of Jesus Christ. Mondo was deeply entrenched in a dark world that most Christians have never encountered, and after reading his story, I better understand why Mondo demonstrates such gratefulness for what God has done in his life—as well as thankfulness to the people who played a role in his amazing transformation. If anyone is searching for hope or knows someone who needs hope, this is the book they should reach for because it demonstrates the living hope that God can change anyone's life!

—RICK RENNER
MINISTER; AUTHOR; BROADCASTER

My Crazy Life will bring hope to any soul. My dear brother Mondo's real-life story from a gangbanging gangster to a son saved by grace is profound evidence of how God's great love, power, and grace can save and transform any life.

—DARRYL STRAWBERRY
MLB FOUR-TIME WORLD SERIES CHAMPION; EVANGELIST

Mondo honestly shares his compelling heart-wrenching story—how for years he painfully existed, and how he left the gangs of LA for the gifts of God. He is constantly surprised as His plan for him unfolds. And he is now family, and loved.

—KATHY LENNON DARIS
THE LENNON SISTERS

My husband, Mondo, what a blessing it is to have witnessed you write your life story. You have poured every ounce of your soul into this book. There were nights when you didn't make it to bed until 1 or 2 a.m. When I asked you why you weren't coming to bed sooner, your answer was always, "I am writing for the one person who reads this book and finds hope. I have to get it completed on time." This is who you are. Your heart is to help others. You are the most loyal man I have ever met. There hasn't been a day in our marriage when you haven't proved that. Your life, while it may have been rough and at times heartbreaking, has been guided perfectly to make you into the man you are today. You are a rock for our family. You often speak at events or churches about God's purpose in each of our lives. I have known this from the day I met you: your purpose is to change the world with your story. I am tearfully happy and grateful to see that you have found that out for yourself. Your purpose, my love, starts with this book. I am so proud of you!

—Elizabeth De La Vega

I am very lucky. Everyone else knows him as Mondo, the guy on TV or the speaker at church, but I know him as Dad. He protects me, and I know he will always be there for me. I am so grateful I have a dad who tells me every day that he loves me. I am so proud of him for writing this book. I know you will love it as much as I do.

—Mila De La Vega

I am so thankful for my dad. He has taught me so many life lessons. The struggles he went through growing up—he did not know it then, but maybe it all happened so one day he could keep me, his son, from making the same mistakes. He teaches me; he listens to me; he is my favorite soccer opponent. My dad stops at nothing to be there for me. I love him so much.

—Mateo De La Vega

MY *Crazy* LIFE

MONDO DE LA VEGA
with MAX DAVIS

CHARISMA
HOUSE

MY CRAZY LIFE by Mondo De La Vega
Published by Charisma House, an imprint of Charisma Media
1150 Greenwood Blvd., Lake Mary, Florida 32746

Copyright © 2024 by Mondo De La Vega. All rights reserved.

Unless otherwise noted, all Scripture quotations are taken from the Holy Bible, New International Version®, NIV®. Copyright © 1973, 1978, 1984, 2011 by Biblica, Inc.® Used by permission of Zondervan. All rights reserved worldwide. www.zondervan.com. The "NIV" and "New International Version" are trademarks registered in the United States Patent and Trademark Office by Biblica, Inc.®

Scripture quotations marked NBV are from Nueva Biblia Viva, Copyright © 2006, 2008 by Biblica, Inc.® Used with permission. All rights reserved worldwide.

Scripture quotations marked NCV are taken from the New Century Version®. Copyright © 2005 by Thomas Nelson. Used by permission. All rights reserved.

Scripture quotations marked NKJV are taken from the New King James Version®. Copyright © 1982 by Thomas Nelson. Used by permission. All rights reserved.

While the author has made every effort to provide accurate, up-to-date source information at the time of publication, statistics and other data are constantly updated. Neither the publisher nor the author assumes any responsibility for errors or for changes that occur after publication. Further, the publisher and author do not have any control over and do not assume any responsibility for third-party websites or their content.

For more resources like this, visit charismahouse.com and the author's website at mondodelavega.com.

Cataloging-in-Publication Data is on file with the Library of Congress. International Standard Book Number: 978-1-63641-363-1
E-book ISBN: 978-1-63641-364-8

1 2024
Printed in the United States of America

Most Charisma Media products are available at special quantity discounts for bulk purchase for sales promotions, premiums, fund-raising, and educational needs. For details, call us at (407) 333-0600 or visit our website at www.charismamedia.com.

Some names and identifying details have been changed to protect the privacy of those individuals.

The author has made every effort to provide accurate accounts of events, but he acknowledges that others may have different recollections of these events.

I dedicate this book to the following people in my life. I thank them for the support they have given me to write this book. I could not have accomplished this amazing milestone without these three believing in me. I love them now and forever.

To my wife, Liz, my chula—the moment I met you, I knew you were the one. I fell in love the moment I saw you. You have given me the gift of being a husband and a father. I am looking forward to growing old with you. You changed my life forever.

To my son, Mateo "Toto"—life will be full of challenges and tough decisions, but you can achieve anything you put your heart and mind to. Be strong and of great courage; fear no man; stay humble. You have given me so many reasons to be proud of the young man you are becoming, but the proudest moment for me is telling others that you are my son. I love you with all my heart!

To my daughter, Mila "Peluchis"—you are a young lady who is strong, kind, thoughtful, caring, and optimistic, and I realize that the dreams I held in my heart for you are alive in your beautiful spirit. I am so proud of you, and I love you with all my heart!

Contents

Prologue

A Bullet With My Name on It

WALKING UP THE steps of the old Hispanic church building with the faded stucco, I could smell the tamales and pupusas. I could hear the music, the sounds of Spanish-speaking voices around me—my culture, *mi raza*, my people. Past the front doors, there was little to no air conditioning, which resulted in a hot, sticky room. But that didn't faze these people. They were survivors.

I stepped inside and stood all the way in the back, holding on to my gun, a 9-millimeter Beretta with a clip that held about sixteen bullets. I had on my bandana, Locs sunglasses, a white shirt, black Dickies pants, and my Nike Cortez sneakers. People knew I was a gang member just by the way I was dressed.

I recognized the man on stage giving his testimony as a former rival gang member. He was preaching, and as he spoke, he was getting louder, and he was looking at me. I was thinking,

"Man, if this guy gets any closer, I'm going to put bullets in his—" You know what I mean?

A song came on. It wasn't what I was used to hearing— N.W.A or Ice Cube, Snoop Dogg or 2Pac, let alone the old-school *firme rolas*, the oldies—but it was in Spanish. "*Sobre una cruz, mi buen [Señor] su sangre derramó por este pobre pecador, a quien así salvó. En la cruz, en la cruz, do primero vi la luz, y las manchas de mi alma [Él lavó] fue allí por fe do vi a Jesús.*"[1] ("Was it for crimes that I had done He groaned upon the tree? Amazing pity, grace unknown, and love beyond degree! / At the cross, at the cross where I first saw the light, and the burden of my heart rolled away. It was there by faith I received my sight."[2])

There were no smog machines, no concert lights. This was an old, humble church, but man, they sang that song like they meant it. Everyone in that room had their hands raised. Some people were clapping; others were crying. There was such innocence and lack of judgment from everyone. The room had such peace and a love I didn't recognize. I didn't know how to respond to it. A tear fell from my eye and then another and another. At the same time, I was still holding tight to my gun. I had been taught to never let my guard down.

All of a sudden, the man on stage began to talk about Jesus in a way I had never heard Him spoken of before. And he said, "I'm going to get off the stage." As he stepped down from the platform, he started walking toward me. The closer he got, the tighter I held my gun. As he got closer to my face, he started speaking directly to me, as if he had forgotten other people were in the room.

He was looking at me, and it was as if he could see beyond my Locs. He said, "So what are you going to do? Are you going to give your life to Him? Or are you going to walk out of this building and maybe run into a bullet with your name on it? Are you going to leave this building knowing you heard the gospel, that you heard hope for the first time in your life, and just walk away?"

He invited me to go to the front of the church and receive prayer. He challenged me to be vulnerable in a way I had never needed to be. I thought, "Man, I'm not a punk. I don't punk out from nobody." He started walking back toward the platform, then stopped and turned around. I grabbed my gun, thinking, "This guy's about to shoot me." But he looked at me and said, "You know, He loves you. He died for you on the cross. He wants to make things right with you."

Those words would change my life.

My Crazy Life

I F YOU PEER closely into my eyes, you will see they reflect both deep pain and, ironically, deep peace. Just below my right eye, I have a tattoo of the *tres puntos*, the three dots. The dots are small but significant to gangsters.

The tattoo is known as *"mi vida loca,"* which is translated as "my crazy life." In Latino gang culture that phrase represents the struggles of the underprivileged and minorities. It's a way of saying, "My life is crazy, but I'm thankful for it," or, "Life may be crazy, but I'm still here." Each individual dot represents one of the three destinations that gang life leads to: the grave, the hospital, or prison. We called it the "trinity of life." Not everyone would experience all three. We may only experience one out of three, or two out of three, but the ultimate price you would pay would be three out of three.

This was our destiny. Bound by honor, we lived to die and died to live for our barrio, our neighborhood, our people. It's all we had. It's all we knew, and it was all we had left. It was our *familia*. The only thing that united us was our brokenness.

I fully expected to be dead or in prison before I hit eighteen years old.

Every day in the streets was marked by violence. We lost a lot of homies, *carnales* (brothers), *vatos* (dudes), and homegirls. We lost them to murders, drive-by shootings, and drug deals gone wrong. Some lost their lives for snitching, and occasionally some were lost in vicious fights with rival gangs. Let me be clear here: violence in the gang world was almost always between rival gangs. Within the gang life it was brutal. A dark cloud of sadness hovered over us, and a deep-seated anger drove us. Yet there were happy moments. We hung out wherever we could—in the school cafeteria, at parks and playgrounds, and at lots of parties. Cruising the boulevard with the homies on Friday nights in our lowriders was the way to start the weekend off right. We laughed all the time, cracking jokes. Laughter was a way of masking the pain and depression.

To be honest, we were narcissistic too. We had to be narcissistic. We were always watching our backs to survive. I had to make myself number one. In the gang lifestyle the deception of being a narcissist is you are so focused on being strong enough to survive that you don't think about your future, let alone eternity. Perhaps the reality of where we were going to spend the rest of our lives was not as meaningful as what was in front of us.

What's crazy is, although I was doing everything to survive, I wanted to die. I just wanted the misery—the abandonment, the anxiety, the loneliness, the depression, the fear of not knowing if there was more pain to come—to end. It's crazy to even think you can make it when everything is against you. When society is against you, when the pressure of life is against you, when your homies and rival gangs are against you, when you bring shame into your family and they lose hope for you, when you yourself are against you—that's crazy. The *mi vida loca* tattoo represented the destiny of my life in the streets.

Under my left eye you'll see another small tattoo in the shape of a teardrop. It is closely associated with gang and prison culture. In prison the teardrop often indicates one has served time or killed someone. In the street-gang culture, though, the teardrop can represent sorrow, loss, or feelings of sadness, heartbreak, and mourning. I have the *mi vida loca* symbol and the teardrop because they both represented my life well.

In the gangs I was a living dead man. In my mind I was already dead. It was only a matter of time. Death was always near. From getting out of my homie's car to waking up and going out of my house to catch the bus to school, death was at my door. I could smell it; I could feel it. I could sense it. Death was always near, and my time was running out. I should have been dead a long time ago. At the same time, I knew something special was going on. Others saw it too, how God miraculously protected me in situations where death was certain. Yet I still couldn't believe it. I had seen too much violence and sorrow. I often wondered how a just God allows bad things to happen to good people. This question often created so much anger and hate inside me. It was a constant battle in my head—good versus evil, life versus death. Yeah, death was stalking me, but life was chasing me as well.

As you read my story, you will understand just how fully present God was in my life. It's still unbelievable that He would love someone like me, save me from one of the most notorious Los Angeles gangs, and reveal my true destiny. Going from a kid in Central America filled with confusion and growing bitterness, to the gangs of LA filled with violence, rebellion, and hate, to ultimately being able to share my story with millions around the world—it's something that could have happened only by the grace of God.

Think about it, I'm an ex-gang member; the world said, "Lock him up, throw the key away." I was a kid who didn't feel good enough to even sit at the table with anyone other than killers, shot callers, street fighters, drug dealers, and people who relate to the life I came from. Yet here I am cohosting and hosting two worldwide television programs. If God can take a gangster from the streets of Los Angeles and do what He's done in my life, He can do it for anyone. God had a very different destiny for me from a life on the streets. This is my crazy life.

Chapter 2

Mi Familia

W E LIVED IN a very old Spanish colonial-style home with a courtyard in the middle. It was filled with lush plants, flowers, and trees, including an enormous palm tree in the center. The corridors of the main house wrapped around the courtyard and had well-worn burgundy tiles, faded aqua-blue walls, and ceilings tattered with holes and peeling plaster. The roof had become nothing more than rusting metal panels. In America it would be considered low-class, but in third world Central America it was considered upper-middle class.

My parents lived on one side of the courtyard in one room, along with me and my sister, Laura, who is ten months older. There was a queen-size bed and two small beds for us. My paternal grandmother had a room on the opposite side of the courtyard. Grandfather had passed away by this time, but his abandoned car still sat in what was supposed to be a garage, a lingering reminder of his absence. There was another area off the far end of the courtyard where my uncle and his family lived. I experienced some of the happiest moments of my life there.

I always had cousins to play with, an aunt or uncle to give me a hug or tell me a joke. Every evening, we all were together for dinner. I heard so many family stories that I can still remember them to this day. But the most amazing times were Christmas and New Year's. The fair would come to town, and every holiday, we would light fireworks. The laughter when we were all together almost seemed like something out of a movie. It was for a time completely perfect.

I thought we had a good life in Central America. My mother's family lived in the big city. It was a prominent and wealthy family, full of pride and respect. They owned several businesses. My mom's dad was a successful man. He spoiled us, and I was always happy when he was around. My father's family originated from Spain, and he was a highly respected agricultural man who had earned multiple degrees in this field.

A coffee connoisseur, he oversaw several coffee plantations, making sure the beans were of the utmost quality and met the highest standard. He eventually became the president of a respected coffee company in Central America. He understood everything agricultural. Coming from a family of politicians, including his father, who'd been mayor of our town for two terms, he also was quite involved in politics. On top of that, my father was one of the top sharpshooters and could hit a moving dime from two hundred yards.

He was everything to me. I even drank coffee at my young age and pretended to smoke cigarettes so I could be just like him. I was his son, his love, his everything. He took me everywhere he went, and I was proud that he was my father. He played soccer with me and came to every game I played in. He never spanked my sister and me—never even raised his voice at us. So maybe you can imagine my shock when I first saw the demons that rested inside him.

The Broomstick

A s a very young boy sheltered from my parents' troubles, I thought our home was filled with love. Carefree with a full stomach, I was wrapped up in playing soccer, going to school, watching my favorite cartoons, and just doing the things growing boys did. I barely noticed my mother crying in the middle of the night—or throughout the day—or trying to scrape enough money to buy food. She wasn't allowed to own anything; she could not even have house keys. My father didn't even allow us to call her Mom. I was to address her by her middle name, Susana, not even her first name, which is Silvia. I never called her Mom until many years later in America. She had been belittled not only by my father but by me as well, and I did not even realize I was doing it.

One particular night, everything felt different. My dad started yelling at my mother, spewing curses and verbal abuse, kicking and beating her. My sister and I were supposed to be sleeping in our beds. My mother begged him to stop, but there was no stopping him. She somehow managed to break free to the bathroom and shut the door so she could at least get some relief from the assault. When she was in there, my dad was on the other side shouting at her and trying to bang the door down. The bathroom door opened, and she ran out but only made it into the shadowy corridor.

Fueled by an uncontrollable rage, he picked up a nearby broom and began hitting her over and over and over. Covering her head with her forearms, she was crying and screaming for help, but no adults were in the house. In an instant there was an eerie silence as my mother's body became still on the tile floor.

Frozen in shock in my little bed, I felt as though the oxygen had been sucked out of me. My six-year-old mind wrestled to grasp what had just happened. My father—my hero, the man I had idolized, whose voice had always been a peaceful source of comfort to me—had exploded, unleashing his fury on my mother and beating her with a broomstick.

How many times had I seen her sweeping with that same broom? It was such an ordinary thing. I'd be running around the corridors of the house, bouncing my soccer ball off my knees and kicking it in the air and against the wall, and mom would stop sweeping, look up with eyes full of love, and yet with firmness say, "Armandito, don't play <u>fútbol</u> in the house. Stop kicking the ball against the wall. Go outside. *Ponte a jugar fútbol allá en el patio mi'jo, ¡vamos pues!* [Go play soccer over there in the backyard, my son; let's go then.]"

Now the same broomstick she used to clean her home had become a weapon against her. Watching from my bed, I wanted to rush to her side and shout, "Wake up! Don't be dead!" Instead, I shrank back, my body paralyzed with fear. I was just little Mondo, confused and terrified that this man whom I suddenly didn't recognize could kill me too. As he walked back into the room, fuming with rage like a fighting bull, I pulled the covers to my head and curled up, pretending to be asleep. I was terrified and shaking inside, hoping he did not notice that I had witnessed him beating my mother to what I thought was death.

My sister was yelling at him to stop. After glancing around, he walked away, leaving my mother on the hallway floor. She began to moan. She was alive, even if barely. My sister helped her up from the floor; grabbed a towel, water, and soap; and helped clean my mom up.

What's crazy is the night before, my cousins, my auntie and uncle, my sister, and I were gathered in my uncle's kitchen, laughing and cooking, just having fun. It was our way. My sister and I were on "vacation" at my uncle's house. After a few days away from home, we had started crying for Mom and Dad because we missed them. So my father told my mom to go get us. He also told her that when she arrived to get us, she should stay for a week or so. His motives weren't pure, though. He had plans involving other women. What my father didn't count on was during our time at my uncle's, my mom felt the need to start praying and accept Jesus into her heart. Through these prayers something spoke to her spirit and told her it was time to go home. When the three of us returned home earlier than my dad had expected, it ruined his plans. This was one of the reasons he was so filled with rage.

For the first time in my life, my father wasn't happy to see me. He screamed at my mother, "How dare you disobey me, woman, and come home early!" This moment changed everything. This would be the last night we would be a family. I would never call this place home again. It felt as if my heart were being ripped out and slashed into a million pieces. After he beat my mother, I heard him tell her, "I don't want them anymore." Those were the last words I heard him speak before we escaped. Those words haunted and tortured me for years, to the point I said to myself, "When I grow up, if I ever see him again, I'm going to kill him."

Chapter 4

Time Is Running Out

M Y MOTHER KNEW she had only a brief window of time—just a few hours—because my father had left for the city. Strangely, in his controlling arrogance he never dreamed my mother would actually try to flee, because he told her, "If you leave and take the kids, I will come looking for you, and I'll have the police lock you up." He meant it. He had influence with both the military and the police. Threats keep you immobilized because they ground you in fear. Yet my mom found a way to overcome her fear. She knew if she stayed, she was going to die. She had already tried to commit suicide three times during her marriage because of so much physical and verbal abuse. She was in so much pain and desperation that she had to find a way to summon the strength to leave that place. The next twenty-four hours would change the trajectory of our lives.

We Latinos tend to be a proud people. We don't like asking for help or letting others know we're struggling. We typically just smile and keep our issues to ourselves. This was especially true with my mom. Beautiful and in her twenties, she chose to suffer quietly rather than let anybody know she was hurting and being abused. However, things had escalated to a whole new level, and more was at stake. Mom knew if she stayed, she wasn't going to survive and her children would not survive without her. In desperation she reasoned, "Either he's going to kill me, or I'm going to kill him, but I've got to get these kids out of here."

With only a few hours to work with and no vehicle, she had to lay down her pride and move quickly. At this point, after having been battered both physically and emotionally, laying down her pride wasn't much of an issue.

———◆━◆———

Her mother, my grandmother, was a tough woman, but my mom knew she could count on her. She was a mighty woman of faith. Though my grandmother was previously involved in witchcraft and Santeria and ultimately split from my grandfather because of it, God in His mercy and grace had reached down and pulled her out of that dark pit. God pulling us out of dark pits would become a theme in our family. After her come-to-Jesus moment my grandmother was never the same. She's one of the main reasons her generation of our family found hope. At this particular moment in time God would use her to help us on the first leg of our new journey.

Knowing my father would be beside himself with rage if he caught us trying to leave, Grandmother still courageously took the risk of picking us up and getting us out. It was certain, however, that we couldn't stay with her because my father had influence and would get the military and police to search for us. Grandmother's house would be one of the first places they would look. We knew they would be on our trail very soon. If we were found and sent back, Mom would become a prisoner, and who knew what would become of Laura and me. But that was not the future God had planned for us.

Overnight we went from being a family in what I perceived as a warm and safe home to suddenly being on the run. My mother looked at Laura and me and told us, "We have to forget where we came from. We have to forget the lives we once lived. We're going to make new life memories." But how do you forget such horrific experiences? I had to create a different person in my mind in order to find a way to live. That mental separation, especially as a little boy, caused me to get lost in the shuffle of my new world. That day changed everything. My dreams changed. My desires changed. My perspective changed.

If that weren't enough, Central America was hit with one of the most devastating civil wars in its history. I started seeing things that no young boy or girl should see, from murders and rapes to destruction of property and all kinds of violence. There were so many gunshots, so much suffering. To this day there are times when I close my eyes and can still hear the sounds of war. These horrific images only further hardened my soul. Nothing was safe anymore. My world had been turned upside down, and I was scared.

Even then, when we were in survival mode and everything was a blur and the questions seemed endless, God was present in the pain. I didn't know it, but my mother did. The Lord would show up for her—for us—in the wilderness, letting her know He was guiding and protecting us. It wouldn't be until years later that I would come to realize the depths of God's faithfulness. Way back then He was weaving a path to get me where He wanted me to be. Though I've often questioned why God allows pain, I've come to understand that the presence of pain doesn't mean God is absent. Sometimes it's just the opposite.

Grandmother took us to a remote place in the country, what most Americans would consider the jungle. My great aunt and uncle were willing to let us stay with them in hiding until Mom figured out her next move. Somehow she would start applying for my sister and me to become American citizens, believing God for the thousands of dollars in fees, flights to the United States, and protection from my father. Mom would work every odd job she could find to feed us and come up with the money for our citizenship, *if* we were accepted. Paying someone to get us into the United States illegally through Mexico was out of the question. We knew how that was done. Plus, it was an unrealistic option for a mother with two young children since it was filled with so many death traps, especially with a civil war going on. No. My mother wanted to get into the United States the legal way, yet it seemed everything was against us.

America was, of course, the promised land—the land of the free and home of the brave, a place filled with endless possibilities. Yet Mom was dealing with a couple of "problems"— namely, my sister and me. You see, she was born in Los Angeles and was already an American citizen, but we were not. Getting us in permanently and legally was a complicated and expensive matter. She wanted to do the right thing, even though it would cost thousands of dollars and she would have to wait who knows how long to even get an interview and complete the paperwork to be accepted.

Having said that, I do understand why so many of my people make the scary decision to risk their lives and cross borders illegally. So many are fleeing places of horror, filled with gang violence, kidnappings, and murder. In many nations the government is not making it easy for them to stay and make a good life for themselves financially. My heart breaks for my people, *mi gente, mi raza*.

Facing one obstacle after another, including US Immigration Services dragging its feet and making us jump through a million hoops, we could feel the pressure. Waiting for the paperwork to be processed would keep us in hiding for over a year. Because we had to keep moving, during that year, we would change locations twelve times and stay with twelve different families. We never stayed long enough to really get to know them. Though they were always kind and felt pity for us, we never stayed long enough to even call one place home.

The pressure on my mom to start this new life was massive, more than I possibly could have known at the time. I saw her smile, yet I also saw the hurt underneath it. My mother was a go-getter, a fighter; she never gave up on herself. She would one day go back to school and become a successful nurse, but for now she was focused on getting us processed and to the promised land.

It's Time

W E WOULD LIVE in the jungles, in the rural countryside, and in a city with millions of people, even assuming false identities in another Central American country. Even though my mother worked as much as possible, sometimes we were so poor that all we had to eat was a tortilla with salt and lemon. And that's what we would eat for days. When the weather was nice and we had the opportunity, we would catch fish to cook and eat. Then, like clockwork, we would have to move again because we felt my father was close. My mom would later tell me she could feel God encouraging her to keep moving. God would speak profoundly and prophetically to my mother. We would keep pressing forward toward the promised land, America.

A year is a long time to live on the run, especially for a young boy. Not fully understanding the reality of what was going on, I would overhear conversations that made things worse. All I kept hearing was, "Where are you guys gonna go now?" "What are you going to do now?" "What about the kids?" As I heard these

19

comments, deep insecurities began to set in. But when you're a kid, no one's really paying attention to you. No one is thinking you're listening and observing the commotion and the turmoil happening outside the house with the civil war as well as within the family. I was so confused that sometimes I even missed the man I was growing to hate, my father. Growing up too fast, I was losing out on my childhood, all while waiting.

During one of those twelve stops, we lived for a while with a friend of my grandmother's. One Sunday my grandmother's friend invited us to church. Mom was like, "I don't really want to go to church. I'm tired. I don't want to deal with it." However, after she thought about it a bit, she said, "You know what? That's the only hope I have right now. I'll go." So off to church we went.

It was a full-gospel megachurch with several thousand in attendance. People were singing, shouting, praying out loud, and worshipping the Lord. Then the music started fading and the atmosphere got quiet. After a few moments of silence, someone in the congregation began speaking a loud message. As a young boy, I had no idea what was happening. What was so amazing was in the message he said: "There's a lady in this room that has two children, a boy and a girl. And God is saying that He's going to guide you out of your Egypt, out of this situation. Hallelujah. God's hand is upon you. It's upon your children. Your son has been called by God. Your daughter has been called by God. You have been called by God. And every step that you take from this moment on, know that God is with you and that you're not alone. God knows what you've been through. God has been with you. God is with you. God is going to guide you. God is going to take you into a new place where you'll be protected by Him, and you'll have a new life."

My mother began to cry, and she said, "That's me! You're talking about me." Again, there were thousands of people in this church. It was the largest church in the city. We had never been there before, and no one except my grandmother's friend knew about us. But God knew, and He was letting us know that He saw us and was guiding our steps even when we didn't understand.

The experience in the church that day became a turning point and helped me realize later in my life that God had been with the three of us. Mom even had us baptized. I had no idea what she was having us do. I just knew we were getting into a nice pool. I remember my mom saying, "We have to do whatever it takes," so I got baptized.

Let's be honest, sometimes it's hard to recognize the will of God. You learn to adapt to the environments you find yourself in, and you do what you have to do in order to survive. Although it's difficult to grasp, God's will is frequently found in those broken places, where He can get our attention.

He was developing me in this transition of my life, though I did not know what was going on. My mother and sister began to recognize God showing up in different moments, but I still could not. There was too much bitterness growing inside me. That prophecy said, "Your son and daughter have been called by God." I had no idea for the longest time what prophecy was or what any of the church lingo I was hearing meant. Laura, on the other hand, grew fast in her faith and developed her gifts, particularly of interceding to God in prayer. Today she continues to pray and intercede for me.

There had been a shift. Due to the prophetic word at church that day, instead of running away from the abuse, we were marching forward, fulfilling our calling to a new life in the promised land. I would like to say things turned around instantly, but the truth is, our situation looked pretty bleak, if not worse, in the natural. Our paperwork seemed to be stuck in the mud of bureaucracy and did not seem to be moving forward. It appeared as if we could be waiting another year or longer for our applications to be processed. On top of that, my father was still looking for us. On a mission, he was not giving up and had called every military person he knew. Strangely, though, they couldn't find us. It was as if the Lord was protecting us with His presence. Mom knew there was definitely no turning back. The only way to go was forward.

———◆———

When it came to Laura and me being granted citizenship, all we kept hearing was denied, denied, denied. And despite the prophecy, Mom was losing hope and about to give up. She wanted to take us out of this place so desperately, yet she kept hitting brick walls and didn't know how to overcome them. There was not enough money in the world to turn things around. In an attempt to cheer us up after all the discouraging news, someone close to us paid for us to go to a high-end resort nearby for a little getaway.

At one point, my sister and I were swimming in the pool while Mom was sitting and keeping an eye on us. While she was sitting there, a very famous Spanish Christian singer, who was watching over her own son swimming in the pool, approached my mother and said, "I know you're going to think I'm crazy, but God gave me a word for you." My mother instantly recognized her and was in shock that this superstar was even there, much less talking to her. Yet there she was. The superstar said,

"God has protected you from Egypt. And He's going to guide you and take you and your kids to the other side. You will cross borders, and God is protecting you. God has a plan for you and your children; you will be blessed." This was almost the exact prophetic word we had been given in the church! Mom was blown away, but there was more. The singer continued, "Very soon God will open the door for you." She had no idea we had an appointment set up for the very next day.

God didn't just give us a prophetic word in the middle of our crisis; He gave us two of them! When God says it's time, it's time. Mom would have lost hope if not for those two prophetic words. Then it happened. When Mom showed up for her interview with the same guy who had been denying her all this time, he simply handed her a brown envelope with her name, my sister's name, and my name on it. It said, "Welcome to the United States. Your kids are now US citizens."

I want to make it clear, we didn't come to the United States through the Immigration Reform and Control Act (also known as the Simpson-Mazzoli Act or the Reagan Amnesty). My sister and I were not residents but full-blown citizens of the United States of America, just as if we had been born and raised here. The same person who paid for our time at the resort paid for our flights to the United States. That's the favor of God.

On our way to America, my mother had a short conversation with me. She explained the miracle that it took to be on the plane headed to the United States. She told us life was going to be different in America. Then we landed in Los Angeles. As a child, I remember being so excited. A few years later, though, I would often ask myself, "Did God make a mistake?"

Chapter 6

The Price a Few Are Willing to Pay

T HIS TIME IT wasn't a broomstick but a baseball bat, coming down across the young man's chest, cracking his ribs and causing him to double over and scream in agony. Before the swinging bat, there were cruel, pitiless kicks, punches to the face, and pistol-whipping, resulting in swollen eyes, bruises, a broken nose, and bleeding lips.

As a young boy watching from the shadows, the tone of their words and the phrases being used were all brand-new to me: *¡Simón, ese!* (Yeah, dude!); *Órale, homes.* (Go for it, man.); *¿Q'bo, vato?* (What's up, dude?). In shock, I was paralyzed with fear just as I'd been when watching my father beat my mother that dreadful night. I had only been in Los Angeles for a short time, and I was already witnessing another beating, this one in a back parking lot of my apartment building. Five gang members were mercilessly beating a young man, reinforcing the gang code of conduct. They wanted to send a clear message to other gang members that this is what happens when you default or break the code.

The alley-looking driveway had a block wall on one side covered with graffiti; the gang's name was tagged on it, along with the letters *RIP* beside the nicknames of former members. As a sign of love and respect, their names were written on the wall to remember them as heroes and martyrs. I didn't fully understand what had happened to the people named on the wall. But when I saw the beating, there was something different in me this time. A switch had been flipped. While I felt the fear, I also felt a rush of adrenaline and a sense of power—a power that the gang culture called *respeto*, or respect.

I wanted to somehow possess this in order to control my own environment instead of being subject to other people's choices. This stemmed from decisions that my parents had made. Their choices had affected me in profoundly destructive ways. We didn't know how we were going to adapt to a new environment, even if it was the promised land. But even at this young age, I knew I didn't want to be at the mercy of others; I wanted to be in control.

When my mom, my sister, and I arrived in Los Angeles, the gang life was right there waiting for me with open arms. It promised to fill the holes in my soul while simultaneously pouring gasoline on the coals of anger and hate that were burning deep inside me.

During the late eighties and early nineties, the city was making a transition culturally. Latinos from Central and South America were becoming its face. A culture of conflict was being created on many different levels; this wasn't something I was ready to encounter, but I was primed to absorb it.

Life was different here. I began to hear of crimes and see

things that didn't make sense but were part of life in the neighborhood where I now lived. Parts of Los Angeles were inconsistent in that they were made up of different blocks, and somehow it seemed that every block was different. One block would be super nice, while the next block would be infested with crime, gangs, drugs, and prostitution. Within the radius of one block there could be between five and ten different rival gangs warring to take control of that one area.

You see, the neighborhoods were made up of people who had been there for generations as well as those who had emigrated from other nations, escaping their own traumas and crises, just as we had. The only thing we had in common was the fact that we all ended up in the same place: Los Angeles. I was able to walk the streets in Central America and know all the neighbors because our families went back for centuries. In LA we walked around and rode our bikes for hours in the barrio. The difference was I didn't know if I was going to make it back home or die in a drive-by or gang shootout.

Hip-hop burst on the national scene in the seventies and began to tell the story of the inner-city experience in America. But Los Angeles was different. By the early 1990s the city had nearly sixty thousand gang members (by some accounts, there were sixty thousand gang members among Latinos alone), and gang culture exploded there in a way the nation had not seen before. Gangs became part of LA's identity. Movies like *American Me, Colors, Boyz n the Hood, Menace 2 Society,* and *Blood In...Blood Out* were giving the world a glimpse of the gang culture that dominated the streets of Los Angeles.

The nation was used to seeing Irish, Italian, and Russian mobsters, but they had never really experienced the culture of the predominantly Black Crips and Bloods or the Latino gangs.

As its influence grew, gang culture changed the face of Los Angeles and gave it one of the highest murder rates per capita in the nation. In the midst of it all, God was protecting this angry young boy—who was turning into a man way too fast.

———◆———

With no home, we initially stayed with sympathetic relatives for a few months at a time. This time became especially difficult for my sister and me because not only were we in this strange new melting pot, but we didn't understand the language. Most of the Hispanics or Latinos were Mexican Americans who didn't speak Spanish. They spoke Chicano English, or Mexican American English. Of course, most everyone else spoke English. Soon, in school we would begin learning the hybrid language of Spanglish. But early on we were lost and would be for a while. We did our best to communicate naturally as kids do, but I understood neither English nor what the culture was throwing at me.

Eventually, because Mom had been working several jobs, she was able to afford a place of our own. It was a second-story studio apartment that had a living room that was also the bedroom, a tiny bathroom, and an even smaller kitchen with just enough room for Mom to put a tiny round table with three chairs in the corner. Everything was tiny. I remember Mom coming to my sister and me and telling us, "We're finally able to move. I found a new place where we can go and live now. And this is going to be ours. We don't have to move anymore." I was thinking, "Man, it's gonna be a beautiful place; it's gonna be nice!" When we got there, however, I was like, "Where's the bedroom? Where are we going to sleep? We have no furniture.

Where are we going to eat? There's nothing but one empty room."

People who felt sorry for us started giving us their old stuff. This is where I felt shame. My mother was doing everything in her power to provide a roof and food for us, but there still was not enough money to buy a couch and beds. Somebody gave us their used couch, their used bed, and their used mattress. Everything was used. We all slept in the same room, on mattresses on the floor or on the couch. We made it work.

When we needed shoes, we couldn't afford new ones. Mom took us to the Goodwill thrift store. It was embarrassing because while other kids were wearing Jordan or Nike shoes and name-brand clothing, my sister and I were wearing someone else's hand-me-downs. We were wearing shoes that no one would wear in the neighborhood. Mom did whatever she could to make it work, but it wasn't enough. The gang members, though, had money, and they took care of their own. They dressed in the latest style: oversize Dickies or Ben Davis pants, Levi's 501 jeans, Nike Cortez shoes, bandanas, hairnets, and gold chains. Mom couldn't compete.

The apartment complex was located in a rough neighborhood and was surrounded by at least ten different gangs. Though they didn't own the building, one of those gangs ran it. Its members lived downstairs. There was a nice married couple taking care of the building, but they needed the gang there to protect it from other gangs. The gang also watched over the tenants, like my mom, because they also lived in that building. But the manager had to pay a fee—an extortion tax—for the gang's protection. The bottom line is, the apartment complex was controlled by the gang. As long as the managers payed, the gang looked out for the people in the building.

Because my mother was out working, sometimes two or three different jobs a day in order to make ends meet, Laura and I had to learn how to be on our own. When we were living with others, at least we were not left alone. There was always an adult around watching us. Since Mom couldn't afford a babysitter, we were now expected to cook and take care of ourselves. The gang controlling the apartments saw an opportunity. With my father out of the picture and Mom gone during the day, they began training me little by little, taking advantage of my insecurities, longings, and growing hate.

The gang had a family atmosphere; the members hung out and had fun, but there was also toughness, order, brotherhood, hierarchy, and, believe it or not, love. There was lots of music at the apartment complex, with boom boxes all over the place. Gang members would come and go in these amazing lowrider cars. They would just chill in front of the buildings; everyone was just hanging out.

Every time we went outside, I would interact with them. They started letting me watch everything they did. They would hang out with me. Before long I began to feel like a part of the group, like I belonged and they cared and loved me. I saw a family unit. They would eat together and laugh together. They were strong for one another. So while my mother was at work, I was being drawn into what I thought was a family, trying to replicate what I once had. I thought they were being nice to me, but really they were starting the process of making me one of them.

They would say, "We will protect your sister and mother. We will provide anything you guys need, but in return, we want you to join us." I just wanted a place to belong; I didn't understand that I would be giving up my soul. I was only a young boy and already seeing people getting beat up, tortured, and shot in the parking lot; I saw people dealing drugs and girls being pimped out and prostituting themselves. It was *mi vida loca*, my crazy life, the life of a *vato loco*, a *cholo*, an LA gangster.

One of the things that kept me alive in the streets is that I had learned to have no compassion; I showed no feelings. In order to function in the streets, to stay alive, to survive, you can't have emotions. The gang was ripping them out of me. Theirs was a false love, but it would take time for me to realize that.

It was during this time I saw my first act of gang violence, the baseball bat beating. They let me see everything that was going on. It was part of gang life, and they were not going to shield me from it. The beating I witnessed was an act of discipline. One guy got out of line, and the five gang members had been told to discipline him. He broke the gang code, the rules. Even though gangs live breaking the law, they abide by a set of gang laws. If those laws aren't protected, the hierarchy will fall apart. That's why those who broke the code were dealt with by the OGs. Those are the older guys who control the gangs, the shot callers who set the standards for the guys who control the environment. When I say older, I'm talking maybe early twenties. Most were dead or in prison after that.

I was being exposed to a life of drinking and abusing drugs. I wasn't even nine years old the first time I really shot a gun. The gang had me shoot it in the parking lot space where they hung out. As a boy, I felt empowered by the force of the weapon. Shooting a gun affects people in different ways. I knew guns made the gang members feel important and respected, and I wondered, "How do I get that?"

When we first started living in the studio apartment, Mom rode the city bus. Eventually, she saved enough money to buy an old beat-up car. This is what the gang—and a lot of people—called a hooptie. It was an old, rusting white Chevrolet with a brown interior. The doors on both sides were smashed in. Like the apartment, it was just about the ugliest car I had ever seen, and I was embarrassed to get in it. In my young, confused mind, which was starting to despise even my mother, our car could not compete with the super-cool lowriders. Mom was so happy, though. She said she had worked hard and bought a car so we wouldn't have to ride the bus anymore. She was very proud of her accomplishment, but I wasn't. I was only embarrassed.

Years later I came to understand that Mom was constantly in survival mode. She worked harder than anyone I knew and was doing the best she could. She didn't know how we were going to make it from one day to the next. When she was around, she was so tired I often felt ignored. This gave me even more reason to spend time with my "new" family.

Chapter 7

Baptism of the Soul

O N MY FIRST day of school in the Los Angeles Unified School District, I got into a fight. It wasn't pretty. There was blood everywhere. I beat the kid so badly his parents wanted to press charges.

Don't be fooled for a second into thinking I was just an innocent young kid doing what kids do. With so much pent-up anger, I was exploding. This wasn't playground stuff. It was real life-and-death brutality that was laying the foundation for a lifestyle of violence and lawlessness. Remember, I'd already been exposed to more bloodshed than most adults will ever see.

Statistics show youths typically join a gang around the age of fifteen. The early adolescent years from twelve to fourteen are a crucial time when youths who are exposed to gang life consider joining. I had gotten a jump start, and the gang had become a huge influence, which became evident on my first day of school in America.

I was standing in line waiting for roll call, minding my own business. Everybody was trying to play it cool. There were White kids, Black kids, Asian kids, and, of course, Hispanic kids. We had all been bused into the San Fernando Valley from diverse areas of inner Los Angeles to create this cultural melting pot. It was my first real interaction with kids of different races, and though it wasn't my neighborhood, the Valley was heavily influenced by gang activity.

I knew I was being watched and evaluated in this new environment. There were gangs representing each of the races. Although considered safer than the rest of Los Angeles, the Sunland-Tujunga neighborhood in the San Fernando Valley, where my school was located, was known in the nineties for its biker gangs but later became home to seventy-eight gangs and fifteen thousand gang members that were known to law enforcement.

Beginning with the bus ride, school was a war zone of rival gangs. At that time, I had not been officially jumped into the gang, but I was already being associated with it. And what I had learned is that if someone messes with you, you do not hesitate to fight. I was already the perfect candidate to be in the gang. Nobody pushed me around or punked me.

Everyone standing in line was speaking English, and I didn't know the language. This kid turned around and said something to me that I couldn't understand. He kept saying it over and over, and I was looking at him with this confused look on my face. Meanwhile, every other kid in line was laughing at me. Another guy standing next to me looked Hispanic. I didn't know if he spoke Spanish or not, because not everybody who looks Hispanic speaks Spanish. I took a chance and asked, "What did he say?" He turned and looked at me like a deer in headlights. "Tell me," I demanded again. "What'd he say about me?"

He repeated in Spanish what the kid had said in English. Let's just say he wasn't inviting me to his birthday party. There were a lot of profanities mixed in. I took my backpack off, reached back with everything I had in me, and punched this kid in the face, shattering his nose. I didn't let up until the teacher peeled me off him. He was shocked, as was most everyone else. Nobody saw it coming, especially from this skinny little Hispanic boy who didn't even know how to fight. That day I looked like I did.

That was the first day I let everybody know, "You're not gonna mess with me." But it was also the day I ended up with my first major problem because, as I said, I beat this kid so badly his parents wanted to press charges. Now I was sitting in the principal's office, waiting for the police to arrive.

Before they showed up, however, the teacher who had pulled me off the boy came in, another sign that God's hand of protection and grace was on me. This teacher, who I'll forever be grateful for, knew I didn't speak English and that I was frustrated. A button had been pushed. He told the principal, "I see potential in him, something great. Let me work with him." When nobody else could, he was able to see past where I was in that moment. He saw the great person I could become. Thank God for good teachers, especially the ones in the war zones. He convinced the principal not to send me to jail and promised to work with me. This teacher did just that and instilled in me some critical values that I would carry throughout my life. Yet it wasn't enough to keep me away from the gang pressure.

Lurking in the background, the gang recruiters in my

neighborhood and at school never stopped watching me. They wanted to see if I had what it took to become one of them. Being accepted wasn't so much in how you dressed but in the way you carried yourself, the way you talked, whether you looked tough and intimidating to the opposition, and, most importantly, whether you could back up that tough exterior. The gang could dress you up in gold chains and Dickies later.

If you were a candidate, you would get tested to see if you had the heart to represent your brothers and protect the territory, the neighborhood. If you backed down from representing where you were from and didn't fight, you would become ostracized. You would get the "green light" label, which meant you were fair game to be beaten up at any moment. You were then known as weak, a laughingstock of the neighborhood. They would never trust you and would either shoot you or set you up to be put in jail. It was brutal, and the pressure was unrelenting.

Word had gotten around school and the apartment complex about how I had messed up the boy's nose. I had passed the initial test. The OGs and homies knew I was for real and treated me like a little brother. Still, the most severe test for jumping into the gang and becoming an official member was yet to come. I'm talking about initiation—*the baptism of the soul.*

I call it the baptism of the soul because this initiation doesn't just make you a member; it transforms you at the core of your being. You go into it with one identity and come out with another. If you pass the test, you even get tagged with a new name—a gang nickname. You're giving up something— your soul—in order to become something else. The catch is, it's what *they* want you to become, what they expect you to be—all in the name of respect and brotherhood.

From a purely physical standpoint, the baptism of the soul is about allowing yourself to get beaten up by your own gang. Your brothers will beat you down to the point that you're close to death. I'm talking about sixteen-to-twenty-year-olds beating up eleven-, twelve-, and thirteen-year-olds. The initiation is to see if you can handle a beating from a rival gang. They want you to feel the pain that was about to be introduced to you in the streets. You had to understand that the beating you were receiving was the type of beating you would get from rival gang members or the police.

So four or five guys from your own gang would unleash every ounce of their strength on you, hitting you with their fists, kicking you in the ribs, and punching you in the head. You're being bruised and your bones are being broken to the point that some have ended up in the hospital for several days. But you come out of it a gang member. When the beating is over, you've become a man. Before the beating, you have the eyes of an innocent child. By the time the beating is over, your eyes have been filled with anger and hate. The way you stand, walk, carry yourself—it all changes. You start off looking like a scared little puppy. By the time they are finished with you, you look like a fierce wolf.

They tell you, "From this moment on, your duty is to live and die for the neighborhood, for the gang." Every ounce of your dignity, strength, and pride is drawn upon during that initiation. That pride is what sustains you through the pain and torture. It's the baptism of the soul because in that short amount of time—seconds—you go from being a boy to being a man. If you pass the test and are broken into the gang, that seed of pride you were born with becomes narcissistic pride. You feel powerful, invincible. You think, "If I survived this, no one can touch me."

The Making of an
LA Gangster

WAS ELEVEN WHEN I had my baptism of the soul. Four teenage guys were picked out of the gang to initiate me. They circled me while I braced myself. It didn't matter what physical stance I took in an attempt to defend myself; the punches and kicks were coming from every direction, and the only thing I could do was cover my head and hope my face wasn't hit. I kept thinking I had to protect my face from cuts and bruises, a broken nose, or broken teeth. And I wanted to avoid a concussion or something worse, like death from a blow to the head.

I was crying inside from the pain, but I did not express it. It was the first time my body had been violated by human flesh, and I didn't know if I was dying and needed to cry out, "Help! Stop!" or hold it in. All I knew as the numbness and shock began to set in was that I could not let my feelings out in front of these guys. These were killers who didn't hesitate to throw a punch or pull a trigger. Trained gangsters of the streets, many would end up as lifers in prison or dead.

As the assault came to an end, so did every ounce of my innocence. When I finally attempted to pull myself up from the hard, cold concrete, I could barely move. They embraced me and brought me up. Dazed and confused, I didn't know where I was. Stars were circling in my spinning head as the numbness was being replaced by pain—searing, throbbing pain. I had bruises everywhere, and my face was swollen. It felt as though my ribs were broken. This baptism felt as if it lasted a lifetime when in reality it lasted only seconds. People say your life can change in a day. But it doesn't always take twenty-four hours. You can lose who you are in seconds.

As I was coming to my senses, I heard cheering. "You're one of us, homie!" "You're down like James Brown, *ese*." "*Órale,* little *vato*. [Go for it, little dude.]" "*Bienvenido a la clika,* homie! [Welcome to the clique, homie!] You can't go back now!" Pride started rising up inside me. I was now introduced to a new way of communicating by using hand signs, special slang, or words with hidden messages. I did not realize it then, but the gang I was now part of was considered the biggest and deadliest street gang to rise from the nation's gang capital, reshaping Los Angeles' criminal underworld.

With as many as twenty thousand members throughout Southern California alone, the gang was twenty times the size of the region's typical gang, dwarfing even the notorious Black gangs, such as the Crips and the Bloods. It was recognized as one of the most violent and prolific street gangs in the United States. Although primarily Latino, the gang had broken with tradition and opened its ranks to people of all races from many working-class neighborhoods in a calculated move to boost its numbers. Its primary recruitment targets were young immigrants.

The gang I was now part of had been known for leaving a bloody trail in the city of Los Angeles since 1990 at a pace three times that of many of the city's most active gangs. It also pioneered a disturbing trend in gangs: renting street corners—sometimes in hourly shifts—to non-gang dope peddlers, who are forced to pay "taxes." One gang expert said our gang was worse than cancer. A cancer you can kill. These guys keep growing and are full of vengeance.

The gang's central nervous system consisted of older members—*veteranos*—who oversee a loose-knit network of cliques whose members share an intense loyalty to the gang's values and ambitions. With this as my new family, I felt indestructible, as though nothing could stop me and I could take on the world. My job from that moment on was to live up to the three Rs of gang culture: reputation, respect, and retaliation. My motto became "I live to die and die to live for the hood."

They nicknamed me Danger (Peligroso) because I was able to move around in areas no one expected me to move around in. I was able to pretend to be someone innocent when I wasn't. They saw that as a weapon. To them my age and size were a tool, not a weakness. I had the aura, the attitude, and the vibe, yet I didn't quite dress like the others. I couldn't afford the gear it took to look like a *cholo*, a gang member—yet. They said, "We can put this guy over here as a chameleon because he don't look like one of us. Yet he acts like one of us. He has our heart. So we can put him over there, and no one will ever know that he's one of us."

When they named me Danger, everything changed. It was then that the streets began to call me. The streets became my family, and my values became the streets' values. My thoughts became the streets' thoughts. My identity became the false identity the streets give you. The streets became my home away from home.

Obviously I wanted to be a strong survivor on the streets and live up to my name, Danger. Yet I was also trying to hide my gang activity from my mother and sister. Not only did my baptism of the soul transform me, but it was also going to expose me. Being associated with the gang in the street and still being little Mondo at home was going to become a difficult balance to maintain. Actually, it would be an impossible balance to maintain.

Chapter 9

A Deadly Combination

NOW HAD A new name and a new purpose, Peligroso—Danger. Even though I looked anything but dangerous, I was determined to live up to my new tag.

What you have to really grasp here is that in the beginning I didn't look like a gang member. I looked like a little eleven-year-old Hispanic boy, yet I was growing increasingly rebellious. As I said, I didn't fit the typical gangster mold. The more the gang used me as a chameleon, the more respect I earned. In the beginning stages as a pewee, I was used as a delivery boy, dropping off brown paper bags filled with drugs or money. I was used to tag walls because of my art skills. As I started developing, I became a recruiter at school, selling small sacks of all types of drugs, eight balls or what we called nickel-and-dimes.

Everyone in the gang had street corners assigned to them, and as I started to progress, my homeboy and I were also put in charge of a street corner. Every spot had to generate a certain amount of money, and we could keep whatever was left.

We were playing cat and mouse against the police, knowing an undercover cop would infiltrate and bring you down. I had a plan and strategically worked on it so we wouldn't get caught. Let's just say we never were seen handling or selling the products directly. We put others to work for us, and it was working. The money was coming in, not Pablo Escobar type of money, but it was very fruitful for some boys who just managed to execute a plan the right way. Our corner was making money and keeping the OGs happy and off our backs, which was key when it came to growth.

For me, work was always first. I never got hooked on drugs. I did not like drugs. I tried them here and there but not as often as you'd expect. I did not want to lose control of my life. Plus, I did not like what drugs were doing to my friends, my homies. They became addicts and started overdosing from the pureness of crack cocaine and other hardcore drugs. Instead of using drugs, I sold them. I gained status quickly in my clique. My assignments included collecting taxes from drug dealers at the corners and storefronts in exchange for protection, stealing cars, fighting to defend and expand our territory, participating in shoot-outs, and fighting rival gangs at school. I had to help set a precedent that we were in control. Defending our territories from rival gangs and representing our gang was my constant assignment, regardless of the cost.

As time passed, it was inevitable that the reality of my being a gang member would get exposed at home. Yet I was less concerned about it as my arrogance grew. I went from having hair to shaving my head. Money started flowing through my hands as a result of my assignments, so I started dressing to fit who I was becoming. My first big purchase was a beautiful diamond Rolex. At the time, there were commercials airing on television warning parents that if your son is acting a certain way, he may be a gang member. If your son is wearing certain clothes or talking a particular way, he may be a gang member. Be careful when you see this or that behavior because it means your son has likely fallen into the trap of gang life.

All of the above was true with me. In those early days, to keep my identity secret from my mother, I would leave home dressed innocently, but somewhere on the way to school I would change into my gang attire. My homies were doing the same thing. After a while I started ditching school altogether. When I hopped off the bus, one of my homies would pick me up in a lowrider, and we'd take care of a few business matters or go and recruit. On other days, we just cruised around or hung out and partied. We called these "ditching parties." School buses and school were merely contact points for the gang life.

Gaining respect while advancing up the hierarchy was fueling my sense of power. What's crazy is, at the same time, I was boiling with anger and feelings of abandonment, trying to figure out why I was even in a gang. Narcissism and pain are a deadly combination that can set you down an endless path of trying to prove your self-worth. I always wondered if I was doing something wrong. I know now that my father sent police searching for us in Central America, but back then, I had no idea. So I wondered, "Was it my fault that my father and mother left each other? Was I not good enough to be wanted?" These thoughts consumed me.

Long before my formal initiation, the gangs had started robbing my soul. The baptism merely sealed it. And when the gang life steals your soul, you get blinders on your eyes so you can't see anything but what the gang wants you to see, what they are promising. But it's a false romance that leaves you empty while keeping you straining for more. They stole my soul to the point that I didn't even know who my real family was anymore. I saw individuals die at a young age. I watched them get stabbed and beaten and their heads blown off right in front of me. It was horrendous, and it stunned me that someone could take a person's life and not even blink.

Each time I witnessed an act of violence, starting with my father beating my mother, my own heart hardened a bit more until eventually it was a stone-cold rock. I started believing this was the way it was supposed to be. I had to figure out how to survive while advancing as a gangster. At the same time, my inner young man was crying out for help, screaming silently, "Why doesn't anyone hear me?"

Yet despite the turmoil churning inside me, I was all in. And once you're in the gang, getting out is next to impossible. You belong to them. It would take a miracle to break free. Fortunately, God is all about miracles. Though it would take several more years, that's exactly what I would get. He would intervene in an unexpected way. There would be even more prophetic words. Even in the midst of my rebellion and hardness of heart, God was working His perfect will in me as I navigated the new, jagged wilderness of gang life.

God never created us to be gangsters, drug dealers, addicts, pimps, or hustlers. That identity is taken on in order to survive the street environment. Many of my fellow gang members were trying to escape their own abusive and fatherless situations. It is worth noting that a high percentage—as much as 85 percent by some accounts—come from fatherless homes, and many are exposed to violence or abuse at a young age. The behavior on the streets is not justified or excused, but the reality is that hurt people hurt people. Most of the gang members have anger stemming from deep wounds of betrayal and abandonment.

After a while my mother just felt overwhelmed and didn't know what to do with me or how to handle me. Eventually, when she felt the environment was getting too crazy, Mom actually took a bold step and moved us to another apartment in another neighborhood. It was close to a community college, and the building was a little nicer than the previous one. We were moving up in the world. This apartment had one bedroom, but it was a nice place with more space and better furniture.

We no longer had to live on top of each other. The building was clean and secure, and the people who lived there all seemed like decent people. There was no gang activity in that building except for me. There was a courtyard, which meant I had room to kick the ball just as I had done back home in Central America. Instead of making Mom mad, I would drive the tenants crazy with the sound of the ball.

Unfortunately I was too entrenched in my dangerous life, and our new apartment was located smack in the middle of rival gang territory. I was surrounded by enemies of my own gang. And you didn't dare switch gangs. To do so was a death sentence. Like fighting a war in a foreign country populated with hostile forces, every day I had to navigate through enemy zones of rival Black and Hispanic gangs. It was intense because at that time in the nineties, the big LA riots had begun to take place. Those riots caused a commotion around my neighborhood, forcing me to be involved. Simultaneously I had to be at home protecting my building from break-ins. It was an unbelievable time because of the theft, looting, fires, gang fighting, and police brutality taking place. Everything was happening all around us, yet we had to protect our own environment.

⬤

The more defiant I was becoming, the more my mother and I butted heads. I was hurting her in many of the ways my father had hurt her. The pain I inflicted wasn't physical but emotional. I had become detached from home. I was so angry at her, yet I didn't understand why. I was dealing with abandonment, depression, and self-identity issues. I couldn't say anything or let anyone find out what I was feeling. It would be considered a sign of weakness, and that could be used against me by someone in my gang. My mother was worried that one day she was going to receive a call that her son had been killed. That was something I thought about every single day. But I didn't realize Mom was scared not only for my safety but also for my sister's and her own.

It all came to a head one day when she gave me an ultimatum: "I don't want you in my house. I cannot have this gang violence, and I cannot have a gang member living in my house." Fine by me. I didn't want anything to do with her, or any of my family members, for that matter.

I had so much hate, and I didn't know why. My mom had done everything she could to support my sister and me, but I didn't want to be seen with her. I was ashamed of her. She was constantly telling me that I reminded her of my father, and I began to feel a resentment toward my mother that I couldn't explain.

I walked into the apartment to get my stuff and found out that I didn't have anything left. She had given away my clothes!

My Jordans, my Dickies, my Nike Cortezes—they were all gone. She had given away every expensive thing I owned. Alone in the apartment, seeing my things gone, it hit me how I had hurt my mother. I looked at myself and didn't recognize who I was anymore. But I didn't know how to change.

I think the question that haunted me was, If people knew the real me, would they still consider me the gang member they had seen? If people knew the real me, would they still consider me their homeboy? The false identity I had created had to be fed by false love. In the gang we didn't have real love. It was real enough to carry us through the next day, but it wasn't enough to fill the void.

There were a lot of us in the gang who felt something was missing in our lives, yet we didn't know how to communicate what we were looking for. We had to portray this false image of strength because that's what it meant to be a pillar of the gang. Yet inside we were broken, dealing with depression, anxiety, and shame. Behind the door we kept tightly closed, there was a broken little boy dealing with emotions, dealing with abandonment issues, dealing with pain, and wondering, "Who am I?" So the false identity we created to make it seem as if everything were OK kept us from being seen as weak or damaged goods. Yet we all knew we were damaged.

Somehow I had to protect this facade I had created, and that identity began to haunt me. I was trying so hard to keep up the image, but I knew I wasn't made to be this person. I was made for more. But people were so intimidated by me, they were afraid to step into my world and tell me the truth—everyone except my sister.

As I said, in the gang we never experienced real love because we created an image people fell in love with. They never fell in love with who we really were, and those false identities became as destructive as a drug. I saw a lot of my homeboys and homegirls become addicted to methamphetamines, crack cocaine, alcohol, and self-destructive behaviors because they couldn't keep up with their false identities. I saw them become insane.

My false identity crippled me and kept me from understanding, experiencing, and accepting real love. But God in His mercy saw past the false identity I had created. He knew who I really was, even if I didn't.

Maybe your gang is the people at your job or in the soccer-mom club. Maybe your gang is your past. Perhaps you're a pastor, and you won't let your staff and congregation see the real you. I see so many people in the world today who act like gang members, creating an identity to portray themselves as strong or wealthy or problem-free. They're trying to keep up with this image, but eventually everyone gets exhausted. I got exhausted. I was exhausted every day. Everyone was expecting me to be this strong gang member, and yet my family at home was expecting me to be something different. We all have had people around us who would try to prophesy things over us that God never intended. But we don't realize God never wanted those things for us because we don't know what God's will for us is.

I wore a facade that I wasn't fearful of anything, but that wasn't true. It's a contradiction because I wasn't afraid to fight for the gang. I wasn't afraid to defend the honor and the colors, the turf and my homeboys. I wasn't afraid of being shot. I wasn't afraid to die. I wasn't afraid to go to prison. I wasn't afraid to give everything up for the gang. But I was afraid to hope that my life could be different, that I could leave the gang.

What would that look like? Who would I become? The gang gave me a sense of identity, even if it was false, and that's what I was living for. They created the identity, but I was doing everything I could to maintain it. I didn't know how I would live without that identity. Who would I be? Would people still know my name? Would I still be remembered? Would I still be somebody?

I was working hard to create a legacy in the gang, but where would it lead? Would my name be tagged on the wall as a remembrance? What stories would they tell about me? I wanted to become more than just a story. I wanted to become more than just a name on the wall, more than someone's puppet. But becoming the person I should be—that's what I feared the most.

It Should Have Been Me

I N THE END Mom didn't have the heart to throw me out. I've already said it, but I'll say it again. My mother is the real hero in this story. God was rebuilding her life too as she tried to raise and provide for us. Because of her persistence, work ethic, and faith in God, she became successful in the nursing field. At that time, however, she was worried that her son would be killed or go to prison. She had good reason to be afraid. Things were heating up because of the growing gang violence and riots. People all around us were dealing with death within their families. Almost every other month, one of our homeboys was killed in the streets. We were losing the war, yet our narcissism kept us believing we could win. For me, death seemed to be stalking, watching for the perfect moment to catch me off guard.

One day when I was a teenager, a lowrider with three older homies pulled up for me to hop in. The booming sound of bass vibrated the entire car as I slid into the back seat. The rapper Ice Cube was blasting through the speakers. He was one of my favorite artists. His lyrics, his beats—everything about him resonated with me. The beat was pumping through my veins—all three of my homies were moving up and down with the beat.

Sitting low behind the wheel, the OG driving nodded his chin my way, and we were rolling. We couldn't have gone two blocks when suddenly, out of nowhere, this chilling uneasiness shot up and down my spine. Fear gripped me as I sensed something was wrong. Just weeks before, one of my best homeboys had died in my arms after being stabbed and shot in a drive-by. And for some reason sitting in that lowrider, tapping my fingers to the rhythm of Ice Cube, I knew I was next. There was a bullet with my name on it. Not daring to voice my apprehension, I slid down in my seat and retreated inside myself.

We were cruising down Wilshire Boulevard in downtown LA when my pager started vibrating. At that time, pagers were one of the main ways we communicated. When we got a page, we had to stop at the nearest pay phone and call to get our orders.

"Hey, I'm getting a page," I told the homeboy driving. "Pull over at the next pay phone. I need to make this quick call." He just kept driving as if he didn't hear me. "Hey, *vato*, I said I gotta make this call. If I don't make this call, we're not going to know where we're going."

"We know where we're going, *ese*," one of the homies said. "You need to relax, *chavala* (punk)."

"I'm no *chavala*, *ese*. I have to make this call! Pull over."

The lowrider pulled over a little ways from a pay phone on the corner of Wilshire and Vermont. Now they were all getting upset. "We ain't got time for this, homie. We've got *firme*-looking *hynas* (beautiful girls) waiting for us. We got things to do, *loco*."

I felt in my gut something more than girls was going on because they usually don't question you when you get a page. Answering a page was gang protocol. Most of the time they're like, "Go take care of it. Get the instruction so we'll know where we're going." Not this time.

The *vato* who was sitting in the front seat on the passenger side got so frustrated at me he said, "*Chale*, homie. Let me go take care of the call, fool. You stay in the *ramfla* (car), homes."

"No, *ese chale*," I said. "It's my job, homie. They put me in charge of this one, homes."

I knew that if I could take care of this order, they would give me more responsibility. It was like a regular job. If you work hard and do well, you get a promotion. A promotion means greater access in the hierarchy. I said again, "This is my job, homie. I gotta take care of this, *ese*." When I said that, he exploded with rage.

At that time, I was five feet nine and 145 pounds dripping wet. This guy was much bigger and older. Tattoos covered his body. I definitely wasn't going to challenge him. It wasn't that I was scared; it's that I knew the rule not to disrespect the OGs. But that didn't stop us from shouting curses at each other. The pager started going off again, and he snatched it out of my hand then bolted out the lowrider toward the pay phone to make the call I was supposed to make.

"Don't let that homie treat you that way," the *carnales* were then telling me. "Stand up for yourself, homie."

"If this guy ever does that to me again, man, I'm gonna pistol-whip him," I shot back boastfully, waving my arms and flipping signs.

As soon as the homie reached the pay phone, he picked up the receiver and started putting quarters in the slot. As he did, we heard the loud sounds of bullets unloading on him. He dropped to his knees as if he was moving in slow motion and then hit the ground. My boy who was driving put the lowrider in gear and took off.

"What about the homie?" I asked. "We can't just leave that *vato* like that, homes."

"He's dead, fool. We're not gonna go back. If we do, the five-o [police] are gonna come and question us. Let the dead bury the dead, homie."

Inside, I was thinking, "What happened to the brotherhood? I thought we were down for one another."

My heart was beating so fast, and the adrenaline was pumping through me. After I began to settle down, it hit me that it could have been me. I should have been the one picking up the receiver and taking the bullets. Those bullets were meant for me. Was I being set up? Did someone order a 187 hit on me? I began to question if one of my own had tried to get rid of me. And what about that strange uneasiness that came over me and those thoughts that I was next? Ice Cube still played in the background, yet the beat flowing through my veins was now one of somberness. When you realize a bullet was meant for you, something inside you begins to die.

The paradox was I was looking for a reason to die. I was doing everything possible to die. I was walking into situations hoping someone would kill me to end the misery and pain. I couldn't live like this anymore. I just didn't know how to stop it. In my eyes I was already dead. I was dead emotionally, but suicide wasn't an option. I didn't want to live but was afraid to die. So I was tempting death. I was tempting fate.

I didn't believe in marriage and relationships. I was afraid to give my heart to anyone. I just didn't care, or so I had convinced myself. Still, deep inside, buried under all the anger and hurt, was a tiny seed of hope that was struggling to break out and find true life. I didn't even know the seed was there, but it had been planted. And I thought for a second that maybe it was God who had kept me from death.

Blood Red

I DISAPPEARED FOR THREE days, and it shook my mother up
pretty good. She thought for sure that I was dead. She, my
sister, my extended family, and my homeboys were all out
looking for me. Mom called the cops to search too, but unbeknownst to her, they had already found me, just not in the way
she had envisioned.

The cops had picked me up. Rather, they had picked three of
us up. The atmosphere around LA at that time was such that
if a group of homies was simply hanging out, they could pick
us up and book us. You didn't have to be committing a crime.
The crime was being a gang member, and they wanted to take
care of that. When the cops grabbed us, they slapped handcuffs on our wrists and shoved us into the back of a police car.
We assumed we were being taken down to Rampart Division
for booking, but they had a much more sinister plan in mind.

We were brought into the police station, but the strange
thing was, instead of them walking us into the first floor, where
we were usually booked, they took us to the bottom of the

59

building. That could not be good. They threw us in a holding cell for questioning. We were there for almost two hours. They didn't get any of the information they wanted from us. That's when they decided to put a different plan into action.

They drove into a vacant alley, and while we were still handcuffed, they pushed us to our knees on the hot pavement, grabbed their clubs, and began to brutally beat us. The reality was they were demanding information and trying to extort money in exchange for not enforcing the law on us. They were corrupt, no integrity to their badge, but we would not break. Snitching would mean the ultimate betrayal of the gang code. We knew better than to speak. We lived to die and died to live for our barrio at any cost. To this day I can still feel those batons coming down on my back, face, and arms. I can still hear the police yelling, "You three pieces of [expletive] are gonna die tonight."

After we were bloody and bruised, eyes swollen shut, they put us back in the patrol car and started dropping us off one at a time in different rival gang neighborhoods. They knew that if we were dropped alone in enemy territory, we wouldn't stand a chance. We were going to die. I was already beaten to the point I could barely move or see. Defending myself was going to be next to impossible.

The police abandoned me in an African American neighborhood that was controlled by the notorious Piru Bloods. On the streets Latinos and Blacks didn't mix and rarely got along. The police were well aware of this when they dropped me in that location. We showed respect for each other because we had many of the same struggles, but there was still much competition and hatred between us.

When you were a Latino gang member in a Black territory

or a Black gang member in a Latino territory, the outcome was rarely good. "Good luck," the cops laughed as they pulled me out of the car onto the street and then sped away. I was struggling to figure out where I was, and within seconds the Piru Bloods had sniffed out fresh blood like a pack of hungry wolves lying in wait. Perhaps they'd been tipped off. Those particular cops got filtered dirty money from the gangs and were about as corrupt as they come.

It was dark, and my eyes were almost completely swollen shut, but there was just enough light coming through for me to make out at least ten gang members wearing their red bandanas and hats coming toward me. Through my ringing ears I heard the Bloods' gang call, which imitates the sound of a police siren, "SuWoop! Piru Bloods, homie." Another member said, "Blaat! Blaat! What set you from, blood?" As they were advancing, the random thought ran through my mind, "My sister's birthday is in a couple of days. I'm going to miss it."

One of them began to say, "Kill this [expletive], blood."

"Yeah," the others echoed. "Kill this [expletive], blood."

Just when they were about to jump me, a voice spoke from the pack that I recognized. "Danger? Is that you?" It was coming from one of the younger guys. "Hold up a minute, blood," he said. "I know this dude. He goes to my school. This dude had my back."

I lifted my throbbing head, "Little E? *Q'bo* (What's up), homie?"

"Wassup, Danger? It's me, blood."

Little E was a good-looking kid. The E stood for Eric. We were going to school but not going to school. Some days we would stay at school but not go to class. We'd just hang out in the common area or in the lunchroom. Teachers didn't care if we went to school or not. Most of them had given up on us. On other days we would ditch school entirely.

I had met several African American kids at school who were also being bused in from their neighborhoods to mix with the predominantly White population, as well as with Asians and Hispanic kids. Out of hundreds of African American kids at school, I had become friends (but not friends, if you know what I mean, because they weren't in my gang) with two, Little E being one of them. In the streets there was never any mixture. In the school, however, Blacks and Browns occasionally stuck together because we were outnumbered. I made a point to let Little E and the other kid know I was watching their backs in this way. It just so happened these two kids belonged to the Piru Bloods.

Back then my hair was slicked back with a pomade we gangsters wore called Tres Flores (Three Flowers). When you caught a whiff of it, you instantly knew you were with a gangster. Little E wore a hair gel called Let's Jam. It's what African Americans used to keep their curls nice and tight. Its aroma was distinct from Three Flowers. One day Little E and I were kicking back, just chilling, and I asked him, "How do you do your hair? It looks pretty cool, man. Smells good too." We carried small jars of the ointment that fit in our pockets. Little E gave me his Let's Jam gel, and I gave him my jar of Three Flowers. So I started wearing Let's Jam gel in the neighborhood. My homies were like, "What are you wearing, homie?" They were clowning me, laughing at me, but I didn't care. It smelled good. It didn't smell like the Three Flowers everyone was used to in the hood.

Now, after being beaten and dumped in the rival neighborhood, expecting the worst, I hear Little E's voice saying to his gang, "Man, I know this homie, blood. He's all right with me, man. He backed me up in school. I was getting jumped, and he stepped in and had my back." His words caused everyone to back down.

Now, try to wrap your mind around this. Los Angeles is big, like millions-of-people big. The Valley is expansive as well. There are numerous schools in the LA district. There are thousands of gang members and thousands of Bloods because the Bloods were one of the largest LA gangs. What are the odds that one of the two Black people I befriended, the one I had switched hair gel with, would be in the pack of ten gang members in the faraway African American neighborhood the cops chose to drop me in? That neighborhood was over an hour from where I lived. Little E being in that pack was like the proverbial needle in the haystack. I think it's safe to say God was again protecting me.

The OG who was the shot caller or the leader of that section of the Piru Bloods was called Big Red. His physique matched his name. Big Red spoke up, "Little E, check this out, blood. You take him to your spot. Tell your mama to clean him up and feed him. And when he gets better, we gotta get him out of here, blood."

I spent that night and the next two in the Piru Bloods' neighborhood as Little E and his mama nursed me back to health. For the first time in a long time, I felt like I could exhale and be myself for a couple of days. I walked around the Bloods' neighborhood and kicked it with them. As the swelling around my eyes went down, I started seeing the African American culture in a different way. I realized we have more in common than we knew. I got to meet Big Red again and thank him for what he had done for me. It almost floored me when Big Red made me an unheard-of offer. "Why don't you come join us, blood?" he asked, looking down at me in his massiveness. "Become a Blood. We've got your back, homie."

"*Órale*, homes, you know what that would do to me where I'm from?" I said. "I appreciate the offer, homie, but I can't go back and tell them I'm a Blood, *ese chale*."

Big Red replied, "The door is open for you anytime, homie. You can be one of us. You have heart, blood. Remember, Big Red saved your life, blood."

"I'll never forget it, *ese. Órale*."

Before those three days, I was against the Bloods. They had been enemies, but my whole outlook changed. Later, I would reflect back on my encounter with Big Red. This may sound too spiritual, but the blood of Jesus is red, and He stepped in to save all our lives from ultimate death.

By this time my mother thought I was dead. She had been calling the cops to try to find out anything she could but was coming up with nothing. I had to catch three buses back to my home. That's how far away I was. What that meant was I had to go through several enemy neighborhoods, and I was not going to survive. I had survived the incident with the Bloods and the pay phone, but there was no way I could survive my way back. Unless...

Before I left, Big Red generously gave me money for the bus, and then, oddly, he gave me a pack of Marlboro Red cigarettes and some matches. This is significant and would help save me yet again. Ironically I smoked Marlboro Reds because my father smoked them, and I felt a connection with him when

I smoked that brand. At that time, African Americans usually smoked Newport, not Marlboro, but Big Red smoked red Marlboros. Before I left, he placed the pack of cigarettes and matches in my pocket. "Remember, Big Red saved your life, blood," he said as I got on the bus.

That bus was going back through downtown Los Angeles on the way to my neighborhood. The route took us through one neighborhood that was run by the Toonerville Rifa 13 gang. They controlled the pathway from the Valley into downtown. Then there was another gang called the Satanas (Satan) Gang. After that, there was the Armenian Power, and finally, Wah Ching gang territory. That bus had to go through all these gangs and make stops for me to get back home.

When I got on the bus, there were only two people on board, an old lady in the front and a homeless man in the middle. I sat all the way in the back, and I was thinking there was no way I was going to make it home. Sure enough, the bus stopped, and a member of the Toonerville gang got on. He was wearing a white shirt, Nike Cortez sneakers, and Ben Davis pants, and he had tattoos up and down his arms and one on his face representing his gang. He was walking down the bus aisle, heading straight toward me and throwing his gang signs in my direction. I was looking at him and had no choice but to stand up and throw my gang signs back.

"Homie, where you from, *ese*?" he demanded. Of course, I threw up my gang signs and told him where I was from and didn't back down. This guy was a good bit taller than me. "What are you doing, *ese*? What are you doing here? You know you're not supposed to be here, homie." He was talking crazy and getting in my face. I was in his face. He was cursing at me. I was cursing at him, and I knew at any moment he could snap.

Then, strangely, he looked down at my cigarettes and said, "Can I catch one of those *frajos* (cigarettes), homes?" I gave him a Marlboro Red. We sat down, and I hit the match and lit up his cigarette. Then I lit up mine. He took a puff. I took a puff. Then he turned to me and said, "Check this out, homes. At the next stop, you get off with me, *ese*."

I looked at him like he'd lost it.

"Don't you realize if you keep going, *ese*, they're gonna kill you on the next stop?" he snapped. "And if the Satanas gang don't kill you on the next stop, do you realize the Wah Ching gang is waiting for you on the other side? You ain't gonna make it, homie. The only reason why I like you is because my cousin's from your neighborhood and those *carnales* were good to me in the joint. They were good to me in prison when I was there, *ese*. I owe him a favor, homie, and you're that favor, *ese*. And you got the cigarettes that I like to smoke. I like Marlboro Reds. So next stop you get off with me, and we're taking you home, *carnal*."

For all I knew, he could have been setting me up. Yet my response was, "*Órale, vato*." And I got off with him at the next stop.

As promised, he took me home. This time I didn't go to my homeboys but straight to our apartment. It was my sister's birthday, and man, my mother was so mad at me. She chewed me up good, but I was home safe, at least for now. My grandmother was there too, and she let loose on me. "You've got the devil," she barked. "You're full of demons inside you. You're not right in the head. There's something wrong with you." I looked at her and grabbed a cigarette. "Shut up," I said. "Just shut up."

By that time, my attitude had spilled over. I went and took a shower and was just trying to figure out how in the world I wasn't dead. As much as my mother was worried about me and had been crying and praying for me to be found alive, you'd think I would have received a warmer reception. But that's not how it was back then. We did not know how to embrace one another with love, let alone communicate and validate each other's feelings. Instead, the environment at home felt cold and disconnected. The line of disrespect between me and my mother had been crossed, and we were no longer safe around each other. We clearly couldn't get along or communicate well. She cared about me, but not even me almost dying made her show me love. It was so unhealthy on both our parts. We were toxic to each other.

Chapter 12

The Three Questions
That Changed My Life

I KNOW YOU'RE WONDERING about my sister, Laura. First, I want to say that she is one of the greatest people of faith I have ever met. Her dedication to prayer became the center of her life. As I was growing in the gang, she was growing in her faith. My sister was living her own life. She had her own friends. She was focused and strong, smart, studious, and beautiful. Guys in the neighborhood around us would call out to her, sweet-talking, trying to pull her in, and she was having none of it. She didn't pay them any attention, which was unusual because every other girl fell into the gang culture. Girls jumping into the gang had their own brutal initiation. They didn't just get beaten with fists and kicks; they gave away their souls in a different way. I'll just leave it there.

My grandmother, who had helped us escape from Central America years earlier, had moved to America too. She started going to a Hispanic church that changed her life. Soon my mother and sister started attending. Not long afterward, Laura sensed the call of God on her life, and she began to develop a profound prayer life. While I was devoting my life to violence and crime, my sister was devoting her life to prayer. Involved in Bible studies, worship meetings, and retreat centers, she was experiencing new life. While I was running the streets, my sister was in the prayer closet praying for me.

Don't get me wrong, her life had become complicated as well. She was dealing with a lot of stuff too. Life was hard on all of us. The difference was, where I had found hate and anger, she had found peace and joy. That peace and joy came through her relationship with Jesus. Yet I couldn't fathom what she had found because I was doing life on the other side. Though we were living in the same home, we were experiencing two different realities. Every day, I was facing the real possibility of death or that I would go into a youth correctional facility and eventually end up in the state penitentiary. I knew my time was coming at some point because that's where most of us ended up if we lived. Still, it had been my choice, at least in the beginning.

She was a different person after she found Christ. Her mindset was different. Her desires became different. She was even dressing in a way that spoke to the values she had adopted. Most importantly, though, she began to read and study what most of us were afraid to get into—the Bible. Of course, I believed there was a God, but at the same time, I didn't believe there was a God, if that makes sense. I was not ignorant to the fact that there was a God, but I didn't believe in Him as I do now. I had faith that God existed, but I didn't want anything to do with Him. At that time, believing in Him meant I would have to change everything about my lifestyle, and I wasn't ready for that.

What I thought I knew of God came through what I had learned in religion class, and I wanted no part of that. A lot of Latinos are religious. But in my opinion religious people were hypocrites who manipulated people. There were homies in the street who were sleeping around, doing drugs, committing crimes—you name it. And then on Sunday they were in church trying to be holy. But Laura did not seem like those religious people. At first, I was convinced she had been brainwashed and had fallen into a cult that was using her and manipulating her to give them money. Yet in the middle of all this my sister told me that she and her church were interceding in prayer for me. I had no idea what interceding meant, but my sister began to fast and pray for me. I firmly believe today it was those prayers that were helping save my life.

Unexpectedly, while Laura was fasting and praying one day, God spoke clearly to her heart that He was going to protect her brother, save her brother, and do a work in his heart that would cause him to come to know Jesus. With that word came a strong faith that this would indeed happen. Yet in the natural I was as far away from God as you could get emotionally, physically, and spiritually. But based on that word, my sister contended for my life in prayer and asked God to soften my heart.

One thing about my sister was that she never preached to me. She never got aggressive with me or condemned me. She never said, "Repent, you sinner!" She knew that wasn't going to work. Plus, you didn't have to tell me I was a sinner. I knew that full well. All she knew was that God had given her a heart to pray for me, not to preach at me—not at that time, anyway. In response I would mock and make fun of her, but she answered with grace and compassion.

Meanwhile, things started changing in the streets. The rival warfare was intensifying. Confrontations with the police were getting more aggressive. The homies I hung with were slowly disappearing. Many of them ended up in prison or ravaged by drug addiction. Others were just dying in the streets. What used to be fun wasn't fun anymore. The parties were not enough anymore. The girls were not enough. The money wasn't enough. The lowriders were not enough. By this time, I had dropped out of school completely. Life was getting stagnant. Nothing seemed fulfilling. There was a struggle going on inside me. For the first time, I started becoming uncomfortable in the streets.

Something had to change because everything around me was changing. I was holding on for dear life because I didn't want to lose control. The void inside was consuming me, but I couldn't walk away. A perfect storm was forming on the horizon all while my sister was praying.

One day my sister did what many feared to do, and that was to step into my world. She put her reputation on the line and even risked her life. She stepped up to me like no one had ever done. She came to me with tears in her eyes; she was looking at me with compassion, with eyes filled with hope. There was not a sense of judgment in her tone. She simply said, "Mondo, what if God is real? What if prayer works? What if you have a different destiny? God has chosen you and has protected you."

Those three questions would be a catalyst for change in my life. They pierced my soul, disrupted my thinking, and got into my DNA. I could not shake those words for the next few weeks. I couldn't sleep well. I couldn't function correctly. "What if

God is real? What if prayer works? What if you have a different destiny?" It gave me fear because I didn't know what was next. I didn't know if I could accept those thoughts. I didn't know what would happen to me if I accepted them. Where would I go? What would my life look like? I was fearing hope. I was fearing the hope of leaving the gang. I was fearing the hope of living, of believing something different could take place.

I had never experienced that kind of fear. I'd had guns pointed at my face. I had been stabbed multiple times. Once, we were at a lowrider show, and a fight broke out between our gang and another gang. Everybody was moving in the drama, punching and throwing kicks. When we heard the police sirens, we stopped fighting and started running away. As we were running, my homeboy said, "Danger, you've been stabbed twice. You've got a screwdriver in your leg, and you've got a knife in your back!" Sometimes you get hit and don't even realize it until you stop long enough to know you've been hurt.

As I let those three questions my sister asked me sink in, they began to haunt me. I realized how far I had fallen, how filthy and perverted I had become. I realized I had become disenchanted with life. I couldn't see how wounded I was until I stopped long enough to feel another kind of pain. It was the twisting pain of betrayal. The streets had abandoned me with their false love and false promises. I had betrayed myself. I was so selfish, so egotistical, so ignorant to think I could live without what my sister was offering.

I did not know how to heal with so much pain. I felt so much confusion and turmoil inside that I got lost. I could not escape the reality surrounding me. Where would I begin? I felt hopeless. I felt lonely. I felt scared and ashamed. It's hard to come to the realization that you need God. I felt as though I was using

God to escape. In the streets, when someone runs to God or church, it's seen as a sign of fear or weakness, an excuse to hide. I wanted to get my life right, but I didn't want church, God, or Jesus to become an excuse to leave street life. Now, some twenty-five years later, I look back and realize it was the opposite. I wasn't looking for an excuse. I needed peace. I needed hope. And I couldn't get that on my own. I needed God.

Chapter 13

"Stop the Car, Homie!"

NOT LONG AFTERWARD, my sister asked me if I would go to a church service where a man was going to be sharing his testimony. It's funny because I didn't even know what a testimony was. That word was completely foreign to me. Not realizing the event was on a Saturday night, I told her, "Sure, I may come by. I'll think about it."

Her response was, "No, you have to come. You don't have to stay long. Just come in and hear some of it. If you don't like what he's saying, if it's not for you, you can leave."

"OK," I said, "I'll be there."

"Promise?"

"I promise."

My dilemma was that I couldn't risk being seen in a religious place. That was my narrow reasoning, anyway. Again, I was protecting an identity I had created for myself. If someone recognized me and told my homeboys I was there, how would I explain it? All I had was the reputation I thought I had earned. Whether they're gangsters, CEOs, or preachers, most people will do anything in their power to protect their reputations. It's human nature. The reality, however, is that our fabricated reputations may not be as important as we think, not when it's a matter of finding true life or continuing in the false identities we have created.

To experience the love of God in a real and living way, we must be willing to lay our reputations on the line. The Bible says that even Jesus "made Himself of no reputation" (Phil. 2:7, NKJV). There comes a point in everyone's life when they must choose to go against the culture and stand alone.

It may not seem like a big deal to some, but as you will see, attending this service would become a life-and-death decision for me. Death had been knocking at my door daily, but now, for the first time, life was knocking at my door too. They are two distinctly different sounds. You can tell when someone is angry by the sound of their pounding on the door. Death's knock is a relentless pounding that wears you down until you eventually answer its call.

Life's knock, on the other hand, is a peaceful sound. There's no condemnation, just an invitation to experience true life instead of the counterfeit. Life was knocking on my door through my sister and the words she had spoken to me. Yet instead of freeing me, her questions were haunting me. What if God is real? What if prayer works? What if you have a different destiny? Love was chasing me, and at the same time, so were the life and identity I had built in the gang.

———◆———

That Saturday morning, I got an order from one of our shot callers to be ready to roll later in the day. My homeboys were going to pick me up for a job. There was no getting out of it, no negotiations. It was an order.

It was after 6 p.m. when my homie pulled up in his lowrider. I love lowriders. People love their muscle cars, trucks, and sports cars. But man, there is something about lowriders that I still love to this day. The sound when you turn on the hydraulics, the smell, the bouncing, the artistic representation of our ancestors' paint jobs, the booming sound systems—that was the identity we had in the lowrider culture. Sliding in the back seat, I had already forgotten the promise I had made to my sister. It didn't matter, anyway, because I had an order to obey.

The second I hopped into the car, I felt tension, similar to what had happened before my homie got shot at the pay phone when it should have been me. I was sensing that something was about to go wrong—very wrong. They didn't tell me what was going down, but the two guys in the front seat began to argue about the situation and who was going to take the lead. In the back of the car I was silent because the homeboy next to me was giving off an extremely nervous vibe. Normally they're not that nervous. Usually they are passing a joint or alcohol around. I knew this was serious business, because no one was smoking or drinking.

The *vato* (guy) driving was wearing a black Ben Davis shirt that was buttoned all the way up and a white shirt underneath. He was wearing black Locs sunglasses and black Nike Cortez shoes. Clean-cut, he had a shaved head and no facial hair, and he didn't smile at all. The guy in front of me on the passenger's side was wearing a white T-shirt and had a shaved head and just a hint of a mustache. But what stood out most was the shotgun at his side and the 9-millimeter pistol in his hands. The guy in the back seat next to me—we called him

Snoopy—was wearing what we called a Charlie Brown shirt with brown Dickies and white Nike Cortez sneakers. He was anxiously looking out the window and all around. The whole scene was off. I was carrying two 9-millimeter guns myself—I always carried them.

The leaders ask you on assignments because they respect you, because you've earned a reputation. I knew I was in that vehicle for a reason.

As we were driving, it just so happened, as so many of the events in my life have, that we were passing by the church my sister had invited me to, and I remembered the promise I made. Suddenly a courage rose up that came from outside of me, and I said, "Stop the car, homie."

He looked back at me and said, "What are you talking about, stop the car, homie?"

I said, "I gotta get out. I've got to go check on my sister and take care of something. I'll meet up with you *vatos al rato* [later]."

"Stop punking out on us, *ese*." My homeboys were getting aggressive. "You always get down with us, fool. That's why you're here, because we know you're down with us. We've got to go take care of this business, and after we take care of it, we'll drop you off, and then you go do your thing, *loco*."

"No, *ese*," I said. "Stop!"

The guy sitting in front of me with the shotgun was cursing. We all were. He looked at me and said, "If you punk out on us, *vato*, that's it, homes. You're done, *ese*."

"I'm not punking out, homes," I said. "Look, homie, stop the [expletive] car. I'm going to take my *cuetes* (guns) with me, and I'll meet up with you *vatos* in thirty minutes, *ese*."

Everybody was arguing, and then one of the homeboys

pulled out a gun and shoved it in my face. "If you continue, homie, I'm going to pull the trigger, so you need to shut your mouth, *ese*. We're going to go take care of business. We'll drop you back off. So stop with the [expletive]."

I looked at him and said, "Listen, homie, you can pull the trigger all you want. But I made a promise, and I've got to go take care of this. I'll meet up with you *vatos alrato* (later)."

This courage to stand up was coming from beyond me. I knew this guy. He was a headhunter, a killer. I knew he wouldn't hesitate to pull the trigger, because I had seen him shoot people without even questioning it, and no one questioned him.

Then my homeboy, Snoopy, vouched for me. "Man, let this *loco* go. He'll catch up with us, *ese*. I know this *vato*. He's down with us. He's down for the neighborhood."

Then he said, "We've got to take care of this, but we're not going there right now. We can pick him up in thirty minutes, homes."

The lowrider pulled over and let me out. That was the last time I saw them. An undercover cop had infiltrated the gang and was feeding information to the FBI. All three spent the next twenty years in prison. If I had stayed in that car, I would have ended up in prison too. But God had other plans for my next twenty years.

Of course, when I got out of the car, I didn't know any of that. I was nervous as I looked up the hill toward the church. I had so many emotions running through my head. I was wrestling inside myself, thinking, "Man, I don't know if I want to go up there, but I made Laura a promise." I knew my homeboys were going to start talking trash about me, and I would have to deal with that. I didn't want my homeboys to think I was a *chavala* (punk) or that I had become soft or wasn't down for the barrio (neighborhood). But something inside me said, "Don't look back. Keep your word."

I began walking toward that church.

Chapter 14

The Power of Love

THE OLD, HISPANIC church building on Wilshire Boulevard was only a few minutes away, but it felt like miles. Walking on the sidewalk nearing the building's parking lot, I began noticing people I'd seen around the neighborhood. All the while, I was on high alert, staying aware of my surroundings at all times, just in case I was being followed.

The area was surrounded by some of the most notorious LA gangs, who wouldn't think twice about taking a life in front of these people. They did drive-by shootings that sprayed bullets like a firehose. You've got to understand, drive-by shootings were the norm. They happened almost every day. I had on my bandana, my Locs, a white shirt, black Dickies, and Nike Cortez sneakers. People knew I was a gang member just by the way I was dressed.

It was now nearing 7 p.m. The temperature was mild, not hot or cold, yet I was sweating. Why was I so nervous about some church function? Something unusual was stirring inside me that I couldn't explain.

As I neared the church's front entrance, I could now hear music. It wasn't normal music, at least not the music I was used to. It wasn't hip-hop or oldies. This sound was foreign, though faintly, in the back of my mind, it reminded me of the music I had heard years before as a little boy in the church where my mother received her prophetic word. I heard tambourines, drums, a bass, and a lead guitar, along with out-of-tune singing. Obviously some sort of celebration was going on.

Out front women were cooking and selling food as part of a church fundraiser. On one side a woman was making tamale plates with rice and beans. On the other side a woman was making tacos. The food was authentic and tasty. There was coffee and cold drinks and snacks. The smell and sounds of my people hung thick in the air. But more than anything there was an atmosphere of joy, like this was an oasis of hope in the midst of a hopeless community. I couldn't wrap my mind around how these people could be having such a great time with all the violence and hardship going on around them.

Inside, the auditorium was jam-packed with about five hundred worshippers, and it was hot. There was little to no air conditioning. Women were fanning themselves. Men had their handkerchiefs out, dabbing their foreheads. I'm still baffled by how these people could be in such physical discomfort and still be so joyful. I thought, "Look at what you guys are wearing. Look at the floors. Look at the chairs, the building." I was judging these people, yet they were so happy and joyful.

I kept telling myself to lay low, that I was there simply to keep my promise to my sister. I had given her my word. I was a gangster, but my word was still my word. I was looking around for her and didn't see her anywhere. What I did see were some guys dressed like me who looked like gang members! One had a butterfly tattoo on his neck. He was standing there, and I was looking at him, and he was looking at me. I was taking deep breaths because then I was thinking maybe my sister had set me up.

The weird thing was those guys who looked like gang members were clapping and singing. Some were raising their hands, shouting, "Amen," and things like that. I was starting to panic a little because I couldn't see my sister anywhere. There were others who appeared to be former gang members dressed in suits. They were smiling. These guys didn't seem worried in the least that I was there. Yet I was worried that I was there! I was thinking if I did something out of line or they did something out of line, there was going to be retaliation.

I stood all the way in the back, hoping to go unnoticed, and as the music died down, the man I was there to see took the microphone. He was dressed sharply, yet he too looked like a mobster. His hair was slicked back, and he was clean-cut, no mustache. But he had a teardrop tattoo under one eye. His face reflected life on the streets, and I could tell this guy was an OG. He kind of looked like a skull with skin because his eyes were sunk in the back of his head. His eyes were mysterious, yet they were warm and piercing at the same time.

The more I observed him, however, the more I recognized him as a former rival gang member from 5th and Hill. We had chased him, and he had chased us; his homeboys had tried to kill us, and our homeboys had tried to kill them. "What happened?" I asked myself, baffled by how this gang member could go from that to this.

He started by praying, and he talked to God as if He was actually listening. After giving a few words of encouragement to the people, he did something that shocked me. He said, "I know I'm supposed to be sharing my story tonight, but there's a young man here who needs to hear the greatest story that has ever been told. I know you came to hear me, but this message is for a young man." I didn't know who he was talking about, and I was looking around, wondering, "Who is this young man?" I didn't think it was me, because I didn't feel like a young man.

He wasn't the greatest speaker, but he was real and spoke like one of us. He captured my attention, but the more he spoke, the louder he got. That made me nervous. Again, the question ran through my head, "Am I being set up?" So I reached over and felt my guns, two 9-millimeter Berettas. I was still scoping the room and hoping no one was looking at me. My sister was still nowhere to be found, and I was counting the minutes because I needed to go meet up with my homeboys and take care of what we needed to.

Yet the more this guy spoke, the more drawn in I became. He began to talk about Jesus and how He suffered and gave His life for me. As the guy was moving around the platform, I gripped my guns so tight my hands start sweating. I was feeling heat, as if the room were boiling hot. I didn't know what was happening to me. I got so captivated with how this former rival gang member, the OG, was describing a man named Jesus. He began to talk about mercy and grace. But what got me the most was when he talked about the love Jesus had for me.

If there was ever something that got my attention, it was love. That was something I wished I could have shared with my father, but my definition of *love* had been so corrupted by the way he had treated my mother, my sister, and me. Then, of course, it was further corrupted by what the street had taught me love was. There was a battle going on inside me between my past experiences and the love that one man showed by going to the cross to die for what the speaker called my "sin." I had thought sin was doing bad stuff, but he explained that the root of all sin is when you are separated from God and don't have an intimate relationship with Jesus. And he began to explain how we are sinners saved by grace because of Jesus and how man cannot forgive unless he is forgiven. He talked about grace and forgiveness and unconditional love.

While this was happening, the questions my sister gave me a week before started resonating. What if God is real? What if prayer works? What if you have a different destiny? And here this man is talking about Jesus and describing how He came to earth to take on our sins and our identity. When he said Jesus took on my identity, I immediately thought about the false identity I had created. The preacher said Jesus knew me and had created me in the womb. He said, "God had plans for you and created you before you were even a blip on the monitor. God has a plan for you." The scripture he used has become one of my life favorites: "'For I know the plans I have for you,' declares the LORD, 'plans to prosper you and not to harm you, plans to give you hope and a future'" (Jer. 29:11).

If I was so important, why wasn't I important to my father? I felt so unimportant that it had become an obsession. Everything with my father came down to one main feeling: I wanted to feel I was valued and important to him.

By that time, this man had locked eyes with me. His eyes were penetrating right through my sunglasses into my soul. "I'm going to get off this stage," he said. As he did, he started walking toward me. Finally, he was close to my face, and he seemed oblivious to the other people in the room. He was looking at me, beyond my Locs. "So what are you going to do?" he asked. "Are you going to give your life to Him? Or are you going to walk out of this building knowing there's a bullet with your name on it? Are you going to leave this building knowing you heard the gospel, you heard hope for the first time in your life, and that's it? It ends there?"

Clearly I was the young man he was talking about. My panic, however, was soon overtaken by fear, but it was a different kind of fear—that fear of hope. I was afraid to feel hope. What would it look like to be free? What would it feel like?

It was as if the preacher were looking right through me and realized that all I ever wanted was to be loved and hugged. I had never experienced real, manly, loving hugs. I was never sexually abused, but I was pushed into adulthood, having sexual experiences at a young age and witnessing so much violence and death. I think in some ways I abused myself. I forced myself to grow up so fast I missed out on what authentic love looks like. The preacher's words were reaching the core of my being, and the thought ran through my head, "Did my sister tell him about me? Did she set me up in a different way?" After pondering that for a few seconds and realizing there was no way even she could have known all that was buried in me, the tears started to fall.

For the first time I felt unconditional love, and I couldn't hold in my emotions. I felt compassion and hope. This feeling was weird to me because love and compassion were the kryptonite to a street warrior. It was ingrained in me that having feelings was a sign of weakness that would be used against me. But I could not deny the peace I was feeling when there had been nothing but turmoil. As my grip on the guns relaxed, so did the hate that had held my heart. I didn't need the guns to protect me anymore. Something about being loved made me feel protected.

* * *

There is power in love. I thought God wanted to punish me, that Jesus wanted to get even. Yet all He wanted to do was tell me I was enough and that I mattered: "You matter so much to Me that I died on the cross for you. And then I took care of your sinful nature that you were born with, the sins you committed in the past, that you commit in the present, and that you are going to commit in the future."

When Jesus says He loves you, He's saying He's crazy about you! No one had ever been that crazy about me. I thought my homeboys and homegirls had crazy love for me. They declared, "We got love for one another, homie. We've got your back, *ese.*" But it was all conditional based on how I performed for the barrio. I translate that as madness, not love. They can keep their love because no feeling from the streets, no feeling from women, no amount of money or respect—no feeling ever compared to the love I was feeling from Jesus at that moment. It changed everything.

"So what are you going to do?" the preacher asked again. "Are you going to choose life, or are you going to choose death? Where are you going to spend eternity?"

Honestly, up until that last week or so, I never thought much about eternity and didn't care where I spent it. There were days when I was hoping to die, and there were days when I was afraid of death. I was so focused on surviving I didn't have time to think about where I was going to end up if I died. Really, I was already in hell.

"I don't think God can forgive me, man," I told him. "I don't think God can forgive me for what I've done. I don't think God can forgive me for how I feel. I don't think your God can forgive me for who I've become. I'm filthy. I'm crazy. I've lost my mind. I don't know what to do," I said. "But I'm exhausted. I don't know how much longer I can keep going. I don't know how much longer I have left on the streets. I don't want to spend the rest of my life wandering. I definitely don't want to be a sixty-year-old man living in prison the rest of my life, knowing I had an opportunity today." I said, "I don't know how to do this, *ese*, but whatever you got, I want."

The next thing I knew, he reached out and hugged me. I could feel the love being expressed through him. I knew who this guy was. I knew where he was from. I took my Locs off, and he grabbed my face. I could see he had tears in his eyes. I knew he'd been where I'd been. He told me again how much God loved me and how much God forgives me and that when I'm ready, He's ready. Then he turned and walked back to his place on the stage. And as he was nearing the platform, he gave an invitation to come to the altar. That's why I believe altar calls are powerful. The church should never give up on altar calls and never stop giving the message of salvation in every sermon and on every television program because you never know where people are. You never know when it's someone's last moment.

That was my moment. But suddenly I was afraid for the first time of my future. I thought, "Man, I gotta bounce out of here." As I was getting ready to walk out, the worship team started to play again. These people weren't great singers. These were simple people who had found Christ and were in love with Him. As I was trying to walk out of that place, I heard a voice singing a song that pierced every part of my soul.

Sobre una cruz, mi buen [Señor] su sangre derramó por este pobre pecador, a quien así salvó. En la cruz, en la cruz, do primero vi la luz, y las manchas de mi alma [Él lavó] fue allí por fe do vi a Jesús. ("Was it for crimes that I had done He groaned upon the tree? Amazing pity, grace unknown, and love beyond degree! / At the cross, at the cross where I first saw the light, and the burden of my heart rolled away. It was there by faith I received my sight.")[1]

When I heard that song, I broke down again, exhausted and confused. I didn't know what to do anymore. I was just tired. And then this preacher read a scripture in Spanish: "Vengan a mí los que estén cansados y afligidos y yo los haré descansar" (Mateo 11:28, NBV). ("Come to me, all you who are weary and burdened, and I will give you rest," Matt. 11:28.) Jesus had come for those who are tired. I was tired. I had been carrying a dead body—my body—for a long time. I needed a way out.

As the music kept playing, I went to the altar and I gave my life to the Man who loved me so much that He died for me. The preacher man grabbed my face like a father grabs his son's face. With tears in his eyes, he said, "Welcome home. You have a home." I had spent my whole life searching for a home after my father walked away. For him to say, "Welcome home," was like God saying, "I see you, Mondo. I see you." I had a home now. Years later I would hear these same words by a different man and for a different reason.

No Turning Back

WHAT TOOK PLACE that night wasn't mere emotion or some hyped-up religious experience. It was real—real enough for me to walk away from the gang life for good. I had entered that church one way and walked out a completely new person.

That experience with true, unconditional love showed me I had been lied to and betrayed by the very people I thought loved and cared for me. The gang had me believing I was somebody, but in the end they left me broken and shattered into pieces, to the point I didn't recognize who I was anymore. They had used me for their own gain, and I had become a young man with no love or compassion. The gang would have preferred for me to end up in prison and continue thinking I couldn't live without them and the identity they gave me.

They stole my soul, my emotions. I lived for so many years empty and unfulfilled, just trying to survive, but in the end I reached a point where I did not care if I lived or died. That is until love and peace like I'd never known wrapped their arms around me, assuring me that I mattered. I was free to begin a new journey toward a different destination. My destiny was no longer death or prison; it was life and purpose. I finally had hope, which was nothing short of a miracle.

Part of my new purpose was to let go of the image I had made for myself and find out who I was created to be. "What if you have a different destiny?" my sister had asked. God was answering that question. But the path forward wasn't going to be easy. Saying yes to our destiny sometimes means saying no to other things. I had to choose to walk away from my old gang life, knowing there would be a price to pay. I had never been afraid of confronting anyone, but I knew my decision to follow Jesus was going to cause some commotion and turmoil.

I went to meet with three leaders of my gang to let them know I was done and would no longer be active as a member. I had to show my face. It was the right thing to do to honor and respect the OGs. As soon as I arrived, I started getting questioned. Up until that point, they thought I had been arrested with my other homies who were in that car. Normally in a situation like that, if only one guy wasn't taken in, it meant he turned on his boys.

One of the OGs pulled a shotgun and placed it on my back. Another one put a pistol to my head, and the last one pointed his .45 at my chest. I stood there as other members of my gang watched, waiting to see what was about to take place.

They began to interrogate me about what happened the night before, why I wasn't with the homies when they got hit by the sting operation. This became a problem really quickly because until that moment, I had no idea they had been set up. If I'd spoken up right then, they wouldn't have hesitated to pull the triggers on me. These *vatos* were trained killers. They took very seriously what was happening. But I was also very serious about my decision. This wasn't some fly-by-night religious experience; this was my life on the line, my destiny I was deciding on.

As the leaders were belittling and screaming at me as though I was an enemy, I stood firm with no fear. I was nervous, yes, but not fearful. I had experienced the power of peace and love the night before, and it touched my soul and changed my heart. I couldn't keep that from them. I had to tell them what happened. I couldn't contain it inside any longer. I wasn't going to live in fear or hide it from them and pretend nothing happened the night before.

There was a small opportunity for me to speak. If I said the wrong thing, every bullet in the weapons pointed at me would be unloaded on me. One of the OGs asked me to tell them why I wasn't in the car with the homies. Never breaking eye contact with them, I started to share my story: "I was at church, *carnal* [brother]. My sister had invited me to come hear this preacher. Out of respect for her, I told her I would be there.

"As I stood in the back of that church, *ese*, all of a sudden, this preacher began to talk about Jesus. He's walking toward me; he's telling me about who this Jesus is, and the closer he gets, the tighter I'm holding my gun. This guy gets close to my face, and he begins to talk to me about Jesus. He's looking at me, and he can see beyond my Locs, *ese*. This preacher says to me, 'So what are you going to do, *vato loco*? Are you going to give your life to Him, *ese*? Or are you going to walk out of this building and maybe get hit by a bullet with your name on it, homes? Are you going to leave this building knowing you heard the gospel, knowing you heard hope for the first time in your life, and just walk away, *ese*?'

"He looks at me and he says, 'You know, He loves you. He died for you on the cross. He wants to make things right with you.' A tear dropped down from my eye, *carnal*, and then another and another, *ese*. At the same time, I'm still holding on so tight to my gun, *ese*. The room had such peace and love that I didn't recognize it, homes."

I stood looking at the OGs with their *cuates* (guns) pointed at me. "I don't want to be your age and still be gang-banging, pointing a *cuate* at a young *vato*, knowing he had a chance to make things right with God, *ese*. What I felt is real, *carnal*, and I am down to pay the price of life and death, *ese*, to walk away so I can make things right with God in my life, *ese*."

"*¡Ya estuvo, carnal!* [That's enough, man!]" the main OG shouted. "You have always been straightforward with us, *ese*. You have put in work in the *barrio* [neighborhood]. You earned your respect with us, *ese*. You have kept your nose clean and made us a lot of *feria*, *ese* [money, man]. Listen, Danger, you have a lot of heart coming in here talking like this, *ese*."

The room was quiet and tense. I didn't know what was about to happen next. I thought this was it for me. I was expecting the triggers to be pulled just as they had been when other homies got disciplined. I was waiting for my body to hit the cold concrete floor, thinking the whole time, "At least I had made things right with God." I knew letting me walk wasn't likely; there was so much on the line.

All of a sudden, the OG spoke with such authority it shocked me. He said: "As of today, you are no longer one of us, Danger. But know this, *ese*: you will be tested, *vato*, and you better mean what you just said. We don't ever want to see you gang-banging or representing our hood. Don't be playing games with us or with Diosito [God], homes, because either we are going to kill you, or God will settle the score with you. Keep it real, *ese."*

This was a crazy moment in my life. All I felt after the OG finished giving orders was the hate the rest of the homies had toward me. A few moments before, I was one of them; now I was considered an enemy. One guy started kicking me, and another one threw a punch at me. All of a sudden, four former homeboys started jumping me as a sign that I no longer belonged with them. The same way I got jumped into the gang was the same way I was supposed to go out. They were once again trying to steal my soul, but it wasn't going to work this time. Something had happened the night before that changed my life, and there was no turning back.

Peace and love are a powerful combination. To some, Jesus, the Bible, and the church may be a joke, just a tradition practiced on Sundays or a way to argue their political views. But for me, Jesus, the Bible, and church were a matter of life or death.

Sure enough, my former homies came after me. I noticed them everywhere I went. They had been sent out to look for me and were given a green light to shoot me or beat me up on-site if it looked as if I was representing another gang. This from my homeboys who had promised to have my back, the ones I had been willing to die or spend the rest of my life in prison for. I was now their enemy, a betrayer, a punk. I knew there was no turning back. Taking a stand required courage and faith. I needed God to continue to show up on my behalf—and He did, in incredible ways.

— • —

Immediately I got plugged in to a church and went to Bible studies and attended as many services as I could. I needed structure in my life; otherwise, I wasn't going to make it. I needed to be around people who were stable in their way of life; I needed to be around like-minded people if I was going to make it. I had to change my old ways of thinking, and the best way for me to do that was by immersing myself in this new environment.

There were several people who took me under their wings to help me get rooted in my new faith. One was Pastor Robert, an associate pastor at the church. He was from Cuba and had come out of witchcraft. He knew gangs experimented with black magic and that we had experimented with Santeria and voodoo. He understood the demonic spirits that needed to be cast out of my life and the soul ties that needed to be broken.

He was the sweetest man but was also very blunt. He was in his early seventies and was just a no-nonsense type of guy. In my first encounter with him he immediately started trying to cast the devil out of me. He didn't even give me a chance to talk. It's funny now, but back then it scared me half to death because he didn't even explain what he was doing. I had to stop him and ask if we could just talk for a bit. In the end he prayed over me, and through his counsel I was able to realize what I needed to do to start breaking free.

Another person God brought into my life was a man by the name of Shorty. As his name indicates, he was a short guy, but he was strong. He was from Guatemala, and God had saved him out of the gang life in North Hollywood. He understood me and what I was facing. Shorty called me just about every other day to encourage me, and he visited me on a regular basis. He'd pick me up and we'd go pray and read our Bibles and talk about the Lord.

He was teaching me how to pray and how to study Scripture. I'd ask him questions such as, "How do I recognize right and wrong?" and "How do I adapt to this new life?" Shorty helped me understand the difference between being justified by faith through grace and the process of living in my new identity in Christ. The first happens immediately when we get right with God, and the second is a lifelong process that won't be complete until we finish our race here on earth. There are still things I'm working on. But if Shorty and Pastor Robert hadn't poured into my life, I don't think I would have made it.

Shorty and I would also do evangelistic outreaches on the streets. On the same corners I once terrorized we were now sharing the gospel. People would look at me like, "Weren't you trying to collect tax just a month ago? Weren't you terrorizing us and demanding we pay dues for protection? Weren't you the one tagging the walls last month with the name of your gang? Weren't you creating problems and fighting?"

Just as the community was watching me, so was the gang. They came after me everywhere I went. I had to prove both to them and to rival gang members that when I walked away, I was walking away for good. That meant leaving everything I knew behind—my gang identity, the way I dressed, the way I carried myself, and my source of income. I couldn't hang on to even one ounce of gang life and give them a reason to come for me. I had to show them my change was authentic. This wasn't going to be easy at all. It would take some time, but I wasn't going to give up on myself.

Most of the time if a gang member wanted to get out, he would join the military or move to another state and hide.

However, in my case my church was in the middle of my former gang's neighborhood. I had to face my decisions in the place where I had been seen and known. If I was going to go out and change the world, the change had to start with me.

I knew that if I stood my ground and stayed where God wanted me, He was going to give me the grace and strength to face what I had left. I had nothing to hide. Only people who have something to hide have to walk in fear.

Everything I had earned through the gang I had to leave behind. I didn't take one piece of clothing with me that represented them. I left everything that was part of my former identity, including my way of sustaining myself financially. This new life definitely hit me in the pocketbook. I had gotten cash from dealing drugs and other gang-related activities. Granted, I didn't own a house or things like that. I was still living with my mother, but I had enough money to sustain my way of living.

A lot of people think that when you sell dope, you get wealthy. That's the lie entertainment tells. Only the big drug lords get rich. To keep things low-key, during the week we sold our products at the bus stop and inside the school; at that time we were slaning (dealing) nickels and dimes, meaning they cost five, ten, or twenty dollars. Multiply that by one hundred a day, and that's a lot of money for a kid. As I said, I had to stay low-key; I wasn't trying to go to juvie like a lot of my friends ended up doing. I wanted to be out and make money and party with the girls. I was just a young gangster coming up in the game, but in our neighborhood, guys like us were like celebrities. People looked up to us. We weren't rich, but we had what we needed. The older homies had the lowriders and the street bikes, which the younger homies thought was cool.

But now I had to look for a job. My mother helped me get a couple of positions, but I didn't last long. I didn't know how to be a civilian and adapt to society. I still had an aggressive attitude, and my mouth was running wild. Yet my heart was different.

Shorty used to tell me that I had to trust the Lord for financial provision, that I had to put my trust in the invisible to meet my physical needs, that I needed the Holy Spirit to guide me. Back then I had no idea who the Holy Spirit was and how He was supposed to help me. In the beginning I didn't understand all the Bible terms he was referring to, and talk about the Holy Spirit made me a little nervous.

I found a glimmer of hope when I learned of a program called YouthBuild that the LA district operated. Through the program, you could get your GED and learn construction skills. My mom told me I needed to either go to YouthBuild or find my own way. This time I didn't argue with her. It was one of the first signs of my change of heart.

I signed up for YouthBuild, and wouldn't you know it, the program was in the heart of the same neighborhood the gang was in. I thought, "Why couldn't this program be in Venice [Los Angeles], Santa Monica, or the Valley—anywhere but the very place I just left? When my homeboys see me, they're going to continue to harass me. I'll still have to watch my back." I thought I had left survival mode after giving my life to Christ, but it intensified.

The day I arrived for orientation, I saw enemy gang members were everywhere as I got off the bus and walked to the building. There were three from the rival Temple Street gang, two of whom I had gone toe to toe with in the streets. They were joining the same program but were still gang members. There were girls who were affiliated with the South Side 13 gang, two guys and a girl from the Rollin 60s Neighborhood Crips, two guys from the South Central Piru Bloods, several guys from the Pico-Union area, and some others who were taggers and ravers. There was a mixture of people there looking for the same opportunity I was.

During orientation we were asked to share something about ourselves. Several guys went before me. When it was my turn, I said, "My name is Mondo. I'm here because my mother gave me no option." That cracked them up, and one of them said, "Yeah, I know; my mom got me here too, bro." I also said I grew up in this neighborhood. When I said that, one of the dudes started mocking me. When we broke for lunch, the program leaders told us, "Please try not to fight and kill each other."

As I was walking during the lunch break, three of the dudes who had been my enemies just a few weeks before approached me. When one of them said, "What's up, homie?" I thought he wanted to square up, so I stood my ground and put my arms up. "What's up with you, *ese*?" I asked defensively.

"Yo, yo, homie," he said. "I just wanted to say congrats, man. I can relate to what you just said. I know this is your gang's territory. I'm not about that anymore, man. I found Christ a few weeks ago. I'm here because God brought me here, man."

"I can relate to your story," I said.

"If you ever need us to back you, my brother," he said, "just know we're here for you. And I hope you're here for me." Then he dapped (fist-bumped) me as a sign of respect.

"My man," I said, "God changed my life a few weeks ago. I'm

here by myself. I'm surrounded in my own neighborhood. I'm their enemy today."

"Yeah," he said, "but you just gained three homies."

His name was JP, and he became a good brother and friend. For the next few months, I would learn to adapt to the structure of the program. It wasn't easy; I had to put my guard down (a little), but I learned so much. The program required classroom time for us to earn our GEDs, but we also spent time at different sites to develop construction skills. This required us to be in rival gang territories, and since we were all from different hoods, that was a *huge* problem. Sometimes a rival gang would threaten or drive by to send a message. To avoid the fights, we just wouldn't show up at times. We wanted to do right, but the environment often would not allow us to, no matter how hard we were trying. This was a major test for all of us ex-gangsters in the program. But we made it through.

To this day I'm so grateful to the YouthBuild staff; they were an amazing group that believed in each and every one of us who was there. The leaders were so committed to our success that they guided us and protected us from altercations with each other and rival gangs. We developed a bond and brotherhood that was real. We were all broken and hurt young men and women looking for an opportunity, and they provided that for us. I can say that YouthBuild gave us our dignity back and the tools to function in society.

When the program ended after several months, it was then time to find a job. But I ran into a problem: no one would hire me. I was considered a liability due to my reputation and gang background. No establishments wanted to take on that problem, and having no experience and little education would make it even more difficult to find a job. I started to grow frustrated and discouraged, but I never gave up. One thing I wasn't going to do was return to my old life or my former ways of getting money. At one point I rolled with so many home-boys, and now I found myself rolling solo. It was quite an adjustment.

A lot took place during this transition period. I thought all Christians were supposed to be kind, loving, and forgiving. Boy, was I wrong. The hurt, deception, and betrayal of religious folks was unreal, and the pain they caused me was deep. At one point I found myself in an environment with "Christians" who were very different from the people I was reading about in the Bible. I thought that as Christians, we were supposed to treat one another as we wanted to be treated ourselves. I had fallen in love with Christ, His Word, and His church. But some of the people I encountered who claimed to be repre-senting Christ were nothing like Him.

The last place I wanted to be was around bitter religious folks like those. I didn't want to be hurt by them anymore, and one morning I walked away from that unhealthy religious envi-ronment. It felt a little like when I walked away from my gang. I didn't really know where to go from there. I ended up some-where I never would have imagined, but it is where I found people who truly expressed the heart of Christ. Three men in particular would change the course of my life.

In Enemy Territory

MOM HAD DONE well for herself. She had worked various jobs to make ends meet—from a real estate agent to a disc jockey for a Spanish radio station in LA to a Mary Kay sales rep—and eventually went back to school and became a nurse. At that point, she moved into a much nicer neighborhood. I was still living at home with her, but she was ready for me to move on, and so was I. It was time, but I felt stuck and was starting to get discouraged. I needed a change but didn't know where to go. God, however, would send a new mentor for the next phase. It was the undeniable favor of God at work because there's no other way our paths would have connected—it simply didn't make sense.

It was the nineties, and my mother was just beginning what became a thirty-year nursing career at a local community clinic. Tommy Barnett, pastor of what was then called Phoenix First Assembly of God, and his son, Matthew Barnett, had decided to launch a ministry in Southern California called the Dream Center. Their vision was to meet spiritual and physical needs through residential and community outreach programs designed to support those affected by homelessness, hunger, and street gangs, and help people with a lack of education.

Pastor Tommy and Pastor Matthew had purchased the old, vacant Queen of Angels Hospital to bring their vision to life. Founded in 1926, the fourteen-story, 360,000-square-foot Spanish-style complex was once the largest hospital west of the Mississippi River, with over one thousand rooms and a total of nine buildings. Saving the complex from demolition, the Barnetts would eventually use it to house a massive feeding program; a group home for runaways, abused women, prostitutes, and gang members; a job training center; a homeless shelter, and more.

Thousands of mission-minded individuals would come from all over the United States to serve at the Dream Center for designated periods of time—a few weeks, a few months, or a year. It was a massive vision that only God could pull off, and He did more than bring the vision to pass. As of 2022 eighty-four Dream Centers had been established around the world.

In the nineties, when the Dream Center was still in the building phase, Pastor Matthew was looking for a clinic that could provide vaccinations for those who were coming to work and live at the Dream Center, because it was a state requirement that they get their shots. And one day he just happened to walk into the clinic where my mother was working. After she helped him accomplish his goal, Pastor Matthew told her, "If there's anything I can do for you, please let me know; I would love to help."

Without hesitation my mother responded with, "You know what? There is something you can do. I would like you to meet my son. He has a special calling on his life, but he's having a hard time fitting in, and he is dealing with a loss that was devastating and painful." Pastor Matthew told her he would take me to lunch and talk to me. Mom was delighted. Neither Pastor Matthew nor I realized what was about to happen.

When my mother told me I needed to meet this Pastor Matthew, I said, "Who is this guy? Is he the one that you mentioned started another church in town?"

"Yes," she said. "He's a wonderful man, and it's a wonderful church. It's called the Dream Center."

But I was still wounded from my previous experiences with a group of very religious people. So I told her, "I don't want to be around religious people. And besides, that church, that center you're talking about is located in the territory of one of my worst enemies."

"But God is with you," Mom said.

After some internal wrestling I decided to take a chance, and I agreed to meet with Pastor Matthew. Thank God for persistent mothers. The Dream Center became a major link connecting me to my future.

Located in the heart of LA County, the Dream Center facility would bring life, hope, and restoration to the broken and wounded in Southern California. It would use some five hundred of its rooms to provide a safe and structured environment for struggling individuals and families to rebuild their lives. In addition, hundreds would accept Christ, get baptized, and begin to serve their community through the associated Dream Center church, whose services catered to ten nationalities. It was—and is—an incredible ministry.

As promised, Pastor Matthew came by the house and picked me up. We went to lunch, and he helped me through a personal loss that had devastated me. Then he took me on a tour of the Dream Center. You have to remember, I'm just a young man, an ex-gangster. Why would Pastor Matthew go out of his way to take me to lunch and give me a personal tour of a huge ministry facility? He treated me as if I were part of the ministry, and he was so kind, to the point that he told me, "You can do whatever ministry you want, Mondo. I want to offer you a place to stay at the Dream Center."

I thought he was offering me a place within the discipleship program for ex-addicts or former inmates trying to reenter society. But that wasn't the case at all. There was a building on the complex called Casa Grande. It was where they housed all their pastors and leaders. Pastor Matthew had a room there alongside a Russian pastor, a Brazilian pastor, a Spanish pastor, and several others. And he offered me a room in the house with them.

He said, "There's something different about you. I don't know where you belong, but I'm going to give you a place in the pastoral home. For now, just serve the community; soon you will know what you are called to do." Pastor Matthew saw something in me that I couldn't see in myself. Though I was rough, he saw that I had potential, that I was a diamond in the rough.

"We're going to provide food for you," he continued. "We can't pay you, but we can provide housing and a vehicle you can use. You can volunteer for the things you feel led to do." Pastor Matthew and his father saw something in me that even they didn't understand. They knew I was different, that there was a unique calling on my life.

Being invited to live at the Dream Center was an amazing miracle, but it came with challenges, because the ministry was located in territory that belonged to one of my former gang's greatest enemies. When that gang found out I was living on their turf, they made my life hell. If I thought my homeboys gave me a hard time, my enemies gave me an even harder time. They were convinced I was trying to move in on them and collect data on how they were operating and recruiting. They thought the ministry was merely a cover. They didn't know I'd had a real encounter with Jesus.

Once again, I had to learn to live differently. The people working at the Dream Center were not the kind of people I was used to. They were mostly Caucasians who felt a call to give a year of their lives to serve in the Dream Center. As well-meaning as they were, they had American backgrounds and perspectives that were very different from my Central American, ex-gang point of view. The only thing that united us was Jesus.

It soon became evident the Dream Center was doing something right. The crime rate in that area dropped some 87 percent because of the Dream Center's influence. Instead of just preaching, they served the community by giving away food and providing health care and other necessities. These are all things the neighborhood was not used to seeing.

Unlike in other churches, the main church service was held on Thursdays instead of Sundays. The Dream Center has always been anything but typical. On Saturdays they led outreaches in all the communities around Los Angeles by adopting a block and cleaning the streets, painting homes, picking up trash, and getting to know the people in the community. They also ministered to the kids by partnering with programs such as Metro Ministries, founded by Bill Wilson.

Every Thursday people were bused in from downtown and other tough sections of Los Angeles. They participated in an evening church service and were given a free meal and free groceries to take home. In that service it was common to see a homeless person sitting next to a millionaire, or a drug addict sitting next to a Hollywood actor. It was unlike anything I had experienced.

I was still young in my faith and didn't yet know how to act like a "proper" Christian. I was mixing my old ways with the new ways, yet they were patient with me at the Dream Center, allowing me to make mistakes and not throwing me out when I messed up. I was repentant when I made mistakes, but some people still were not happy with me, and a lot of confusion and jealousy began to surface. People were wondering, "How can this young man have the access they're giving him without even knowing what he's doing? This kid just came in from the gang world—how can Pastors Tommy and Matthew trust him with their guests?"

At that time, I was serving as a driver to escort the pastors' guests from the airport to the Dream Center. That would prove to be another God thing, but in the beginning there was commotion about it. Some people were making up their own, exaggerated stories about me. For the most part, I just minded my own business. No one really knew the depth of what I was dealing with; in addition to the challenges of resisting my old ways and living as a Christian, I was facing physical, gang-related confrontations.

For example, each day for breakfast, lunch, and dinner I had to walk from the Casa Grande building, where I stayed, to the main building. Word had gotten out quickly to the surrounding gangs that I was living there, and a group of guys from the Temple Street gang really had it out for me. In fact, they hated me and would wait for me. We called them spotters. They knew when I would be coming and going and where I would be in between. It was impossible for me to hide from them and make it to my destinations unscathed. This became a problem every other day, particularly in the evenings when I went to dinner, which started at 6 p.m. and lasted all the way to 8 p.m. That was their primary time. They would taunt me, trying to provoke me, but I just kept my cool. I didn't retaliate.

One particular evening, a group of us were talking outside the homeless ministry facility after our weekly Bible study. My friends asked me if I could walk the group of female leaders back to the main building because it was dark out and they didn't feel safe walking back by themselves. As we were walking back to the main building, I noticed that the Temple Street guys had come in with more reinforcements. One of the guys, called Flacco, whistled to get my attention and shouted, "We are coming after you tonight, *chavala* [punk]."

The group walking with me had never experienced anything like that, and it scared them. By the time we reached the front door of the building where they stayed, several cars had gathered outside, and the guys started getting out. Once we got inside, we took the elevator all the way to the eighth floor. When I got to their floor, I looked out the window, and there must have been about fifteen of the gang members on one side of the building. I went across the hall to the other side of the building to see if I could get out from that side. There were about twenty guys at the exit door. I told my friends, "You ladies need to go back to your rooms."

"Do we need to call 911?" they asked.

"You can call whoever you want to," I said. "That's not going to stop these guys. My job is to get out of here and get those guys away from this building."

I knew my way around that building and all the escape routes. The Dream Center had some hidden pathways that could get you to the other side of a building in case of an emergency. So I distracted the Temple Street guys. I made them think I was on one side by taunting and yelling at them through the window, and when the guys moved over there, I ran out the hidden emergency pathway, which got me to the other side of the building and allowed me to sneak out without anyone seeing me. This is an example of what I was dealing with, always looking over my shoulder.

One evening a few weeks later I was sitting on the patio at the Casa Grande, looking out over the grounds and parking lot. It was a quiet place two stories high where I would just sit, think, and watch the people, making sure the parking lots were safe. There was a lot going on. Not only did the discipleship building house the men who were part of the discipleship program, but it also housed the kitchen staff. The rest of the buildings housed the women and the other groups—the visitors, youth pastors, and various other leaders. There was a 10 p.m. curfew, but you could still sit on the patio.

I was just sitting there reading my Bible when I saw an older woman walking with some grocery bags and her purse. She was a nice woman, a volunteer whom I had met before. As she was walking, I saw someone following her and realized someone was trying to steal her purse. Sure enough, whoever was following her grabbed her purse and knocked her to the ground. My first instinct was to jump down from where I was sitting, but I thought, "Man, I'm gonna break my legs. I can't do that. I'm too high up."

Then it occurred to me that if I went to the exit door in the back of the building, I could catch the dude. So I ran to the backside of Casa Grande, exited through the door, and clotheslined him! I grabbed him by the shirt and knocked him down. When he was down, I put my foot on his chest, grabbed the purse, and told him, "You are lucky it was me and not the other *vatos* that caught you, or you would have died tonight."

I knew he didn't belong in this neighborhood. I could just tell. I took the purse back to the woman. "Let me help you, ma'am," I said. "I'm so sorry this happened. Where do you live?"

"I live down there at the Dream Center," she said.

"I live there too," I said. "I'm one of the workers there."

"Oh, I know who you are," she said. "Thank you very much." She paused a moment before continuing, "You know, we pray for you all the time. Your mom and your sister, they're such beautiful people. We go to the women's Spanish Bible study, and your mom talks about you. Your sister talks about you as well. My sons are in gangs too. If God can do it for *you*, do you think God can do it for them?"

"Absolutely," I told her.

As we were walking to her room, I felt different. It was one of the first times since leaving the gang that I felt pride in myself for changing. I had inspired this woman into believing her sons could change. I found out that she had three sons; two were members of the Temple Street gang, one of whom was a shot caller. In fact, years earlier I'd had a confrontation with one of them.

The Dream Center had a basketball gym that was open to the public, and her three sons would sometimes come and play ball. I had been invited by Pastor Matthew to play a few pickup games. I had no idea the woman's sons would be there. When I showed up, the oldest brother, who was a shot caller in the gang, said, "You saved my *jefita*'s [mom's] life, *ese*."

"I don't know if I saved her, *ese*, but I helped her," I said.

He asked me, "Why are you even around? What business do you have here?"

Then I told him, "I serve God now, homie. That's why I'm here. Pastor Matthew has invited me to live here."

"How do we settle for you helping my *jefita*," this *vato* asked.

I responded by saying, "I need a favor from you. I need you to keep your dogs away from me. They are making my life hell. I'm just trying to serve God, but I can't do it if I'm going to be harassed every day, homie."

He listened, keeping his hold on the basketball.

I said, "Your homeboys think I'm here as a spotter for my former barrio. I'm not here to spot no one, *carnal*. I'm here to serve God, *ese*. I'll fight one-on-one if I must, but I'm not looking for a fight, homie. I am trying to change my life for the better. I don't know what else to do. I don't know where else to go. I saw your *jefita* getting robbed up there, and I was able to help her, *carnal*."

"My crew is not going to bother you, homes," he said. "You got my word, *ese*. If they do, let me know and I'll take care of it, homie. If you ever need anything, you let me know because what you did for my *jefita* meant a lot to me, *ese*."

I responded with, "*Órale*, homes; that's *firme*, *ese*."

A few months later I got a call from his mom that her son wanted to talk to me.

"What's going on, homie?"

"What's up, Mondo?" he said. "Look, I need a favor from you."

"I don't do favors, homie," I said. "Those days are over, *ese*."

"No, no, no, no, not like that, homie," he said. "One of my homeboys got killed last night. Could you come and pray for the family? Could you do the funeral for us? Could you be the pastor at a Temple Street funeral? You serve God, right? You gave your heart to God. There are people there that need the same message you have."

"*Órale, vato.* Count me in, *ese*," I said.

The Lord had given me an unbelievable opportunity to minister directly to what was once a rival gang. Looking back on it, the offer seemed ludicrous. It seemed more like a death trap than anything else. But I felt Diosito (God) telling me to go. At the time, I wasn't a pastor and that's what he was looking for. I was just an ex-gang member.

That funeral was a pivotal moment in my life. I had been to so many funerals as a mourner, grieving for one of my own, but now I was on the other side. I learned great compassion and empathy as I was now holding up and comforting men I once wanted dead. How ironic that someone's death could plant a seed of life in my heart. Being a follower of Christ and acting with love as He did was now something I couldn't let go of.

A few days after the funeral I got another call from the woman's son. "Hey, *vato*, next Sunday we're going to a lowrider show. You want to roll with us, *ese*?"

I sat down. "If my homeboys see me with you, homes, I'm a dead man, *ese*," I said.

"OK, I get it," he said. "If you change your mind, let me know, *vato*, all right?"

All week I kept thinking about that offer. In my heart I could feel God saying, "You know I'm greater than all that. I will protect you. He needs the gospel as much as you needed it."

I called him later that week and asked if the offer still stood. "Yeah, homie," he said, "but on one condition: you have to roll with us."

When Sunday came, he picked me up. Everybody at the Dream Center was watching and wondering, "Why is Mondo getting in the car with him? Where's he going?" On our drive to the lowrider show, this *vato* and I had a conversation about God. It continued all the way to the event. At the show, we were having a great time. At one point, we each went to the bathroom. He left the bathroom before me, and when he did, several guys came in from my old gang.

"What are you doing with Temple Street, homes?"

I said, "What I'm doing is trying to reach them for the Lord, *ese.*"

They were not ready to hear the truth. Their perception was if I showed up with them, I must be one of them. Who could blame them? I would have thought the same thing.

"You know, *ese,*" I continued, "I'm not here with him like that, homes. I have a Bible with me. God called me to give him the same message God gave me through this Bible, *carnal.* And it is the same message I try to give everyone, homes. I'm not here to represent any barrio. Man, I'm here to represent what this Book is all about. If God has grace for me, then how can He not have grace for you *vatos* and for them, ese? Forgiveness is what the Bible is all about. Because God forgave me, I've forgiven them—that means letting go of the past offenses for what they did to us and what we did to them, *ese.* What changed my life is forgiveness, homes, and true forgiveness, *vato,* comes from the heart. That means letting go of the past, *vato.*"

"You may have forgiven them, but we don't," he said. "We don't forget, and you shouldn't either."

There was so much tension in that room, it was almost suffocating. Out of nowhere, a ton of commotion could be heard outside. As we ran out, the woman's son and Temple Street were facing off with my old gang. My old homies looked at me and said, "Which side are you on, *ese*?"

I held up my Bible and said, "I'm on this side, *ese*. You *vatos* can go at it. My life belongs to this Book and what this Book represents, homes."

I walked out and waited in the parking lot.

About ten minutes later the shot caller came over with his homeboys and said, "You got guts, homes. I thought you were going to stand with them, *vato*, and they thought you were gonna stand with me, homie. You believe what you preach, don't you, *ese*? Get in the car. Tell me about the gospel you preach, *ese*."

Our whole ride back, we talked about God's forgiveness, and I prayed with him and for him. Strangely, after that night, I never saw him again. He was just gone. The last I heard he had moved to San Diego with his family. The greatest part of my whole interaction with the shot caller is that his younger brother is now a pastor.

I had a long way to go, but I was continuing to grow. The Dream Center became a place where I found what I felt was my destiny. By being there, I began to understand who God had called me to be and what He wanted me to do. But what I really needed was a mentor who could help me develop the call of God for my life. Little did I know, the mentor God had handpicked for me was a world-famous—or, some might say, infamous—minister I had never heard of.

Chapter 17

"Who Is Jim Bakker?"

I DON'T KNOW WHY, but as I mentioned, Pastor Tommy and Pastor Matthew had given me the responsibility of picking up their guests from the airport and bringing them to the Dream Center. I met many interesting people that way; however, there was one man in particular who would have a profound impact on me and the direction of my life. Little did I know that picking him up would be the catalyst for launching me into the next phase of my journey to where God was leading me.

I had driven a lot of guests, but none as high-profile as Jim Bakker was at that time. He's *that* Jim Bakker, the founder of the PTL Network, a pioneer of Christian television, the one who was involved in a big scandal in the eighties and went to prison. His name and face had been on every news outlet and tabloid in the world. Of course, because of my background on the streets, I wasn't aware of any of that. I'd been too caught up in the gang world and bumping to Ice Cube.

Jim Bakker is a man with a small frame, and at the airport

that frame was bent over with the heavy weight of shame. Like a scared little boy, he kept his head down staring at his feet, seemingly embarrassed and frightened for anyone to see him. Wearing a hat, he was hoping no one would recognize him as we walked through the terminal. Unfortunately, people around did recognize him. They were gawking, pointing, and asking, "Hey, is that Jim Bakker? That looks like Jim Bakker." That made me start to think, "Who is this guy?"

Part of my job description was to smile and be cordial but not talk to guests unless they started a conversation. When we got in the car, I took extra care not to talk or say anything that might offend him. To my surprise, though, Mr. Jim struck up a conversation. Then he made a shocking request. "Before you take me to the Dream Center," he said, "can you stop by downtown LA? I need to make a visit and say thank you to the man who is running the mission there."

None of the guests had ever asked me to do that, and my immediate thought was, "Does he know what he's asking?" That mission was located in one of the most violent, drug-infested neighborhoods in the city. It was the Los Angeles Mission, which fed and sheltered people and helped those who were coming out of prison. It's an amazing organization, yet, as I said, it's in a ruthless area. Nevertheless, I turned the car in that direction, but I was thinking, "This is about to get real."

Then Mr. Jim said, "I want you to join me."

I said, "Man, this is going to be a rough one because that's a rough neighborhood with a lot of drug addicts, homeless people, and ex-convicts. But we will go."

I parked the car in the safest place I could find. There were people everywhere on the streets, mingling around the mission. We were walking along, and all of a sudden, people in the street started recognizing that it was Jim Bakker. I still had no idea who he was.

They were coming up to him, asking, "Is that you? Is that you, Jim Bakker? Jim Bakker, man, I saw you on TV. I grew up watching you. Can I get your autograph, man?"

Suddenly I went from driver to bodyguard, trying to keep people away. We're talking to a crowd that started with ten or twenty, then swelled to at least a hundred people surrounding Mr. Jim. It seemed everybody was enthralled that this man had walked onto this street and into their building.

I had been so busy protecting Mr. Jim that I didn't have time to really think about what was happening. When we got back in the quiet car, I asked him a stupid question. "Are you here just to speak?"

Mr. Jim responded, "No, I am also here to do an interview on the Larry King show."

"The Larry King show?" I responded. "Man, that dude only has people that are famous. Are you famous or something?"

Mr. Jim started laughing and kind of looked down and said, "I used to be, but I'm infamous now."

Having no idea what the word *infamous* means, I said, "Man, you're famous. You are going to be on TV, man, and all these people are asking for your autograph and your pictures. Man, you're like a superstar."

He just kind of smirked and said, "I used to be. I used to have influence."

He looked away and put his head down. "Can you just take me to my room, please? I have to get ready to speak tonight."

Before he got out of the car, he said, "By the way, I wrote a book about my life. I want you to have a copy, and if you read it and decide not to be my friend, I understand."

I responded, "Mr. Jim, I will read your book out of respect, but I want you to know that I consider myself your friend. I got you, my man!"

I felt as though I had put my foot in my mouth.

After dropping him off that evening, I called my mother and asked her, "Mamá, do you know who this guy Jim Bakker is?"

"*¡Ay, Dios mío, mi'jito!* [Oh my gosh, sweetheart!]," she said. "Mondo, do you know who you just picked up? Do you know who that is? That is the famous evangelist Jim Bakker. He is a man of God, *mi'jo.*"

I called around, asked people in the street, and even called one of my older homeboys and said, "Hey, *ese*, you heard of this *vato* Jim Bakker?"

"*Órale*, did you say Jim Bakker? *The* Jim Bakker? Homie, that *vato* is a famous dude, *ese.*"

I still had no idea. That same night, I picked Mr. Jim up to take him to speak at the Dream Center. The old gymnasium was packed. They had been doing outreaches all week long. Thursday was their special night when they brought in noteworthy speakers to preach to the church. Some of the most well-known preachers and teachers spoke there. We had famous people sitting in the front row next to crack addicts and gang members. It was absolutely amazing.

Mr. Jim got up to speak, and everyone could tell he was nervous. He had on a hat and was stumbling over his words. Finally, he said, "I just got to ask the crowd a question. How many people have been in prison?"

It looked to me like about 80 percent of the room stood up. And Mr. Jim said, "This is my kind of place. I feel like I'm home. I'm one of you." And the room erupted in cheers.

At that moment, this man who was scared he would be spit

upon and cursed out went from being shy and not looking up to being a bold and fiery preacher. Something just came over him, as if a switch had been turned on. He began to preach a message I will never forget. It was called "God Can Still Use Broken Dreams With Broken People."

He began to share what he went through and how he had made mistakes that hurt a lot of people and his family. Overnight he lost it all. He shared how he trusted people to help him, but in the end they betrayed him. He said he'd been told that he had become a cancer to the church and would never be good enough to ever preach again. He even said it felt as though God had abandoned him, but prison was God's way of getting his attention because he had become so busy and overwhelmed trying to keep the worldwide television ministry going.

But he said he also learned that God never walked away from him; instead, he discovered that all Jesus ever wanted was to have an intimate relationship with him. He talked about the book he had written, titled *I Was Wrong*. His message was life-changing. I didn't see him until the next day when Pastor Tommy took the special guest speakers on a tour of the Dream Center. There was a group of at least twenty or thirty people surrounding him.

I snuck through the crowd and put my arm around him and said, "Jim, I'll never forget those words. Thank you for the message you shared last night. It touched my soul." And then I told him, "I've been where you've been, man." I shook his hand and hugged him, and I said the following words that I had not said to anyone: *"I love you, man!"* And I walked away. Little did I know, those words meant more to Mr. Jim than I could have imagined. To this day Mr. Jim says those were the words that started the healing in his heart, because he had not felt loved after his world came crashing down. No one wanted to be associated with him publicly. *Saturday Night Live*, newspapers, magazines, TV specials, movies—they all created a framework to cancel Jim Bakker and the Bakker family for good. The words "I love you, man" became a pivot point in his life.

After I was gone, Pastor Tommy asked Mr. Jim, "Do you know who that guy was who just hugged and talked to you? He's an ex-gang member; he was a bad man. His gang was notorious." He began to tell Mr. Jim my story, and Mr. Jim was shocked that I had been assigned to pick him up and drive him around. He was like, "Who is this gang member who was assigned to me?" After that encounter, we struck up a friendship that changed my life. It is a friendship that I thought would last only a few hours, but thankfully, I was wrong.

Soon after the tour Mr. Jim asked Pastor Tommy and Pastor Matthew if he could move to the Dream Center. He was afraid they would say no because he was such a high-profile figure getting so much negative press. Mr. Jim knew the media was tracking every move he made and did not want to hurt the Barnetts' reputation. Yet without hesitation they said yes. The Barnetts risked their reputation and ministry in doing so. They believed in restoration not just for the people the Dream Center was helping but also for a hurting, broken preacher who needed a safe place.

They asked Mr. Jim if he wanted to be put up in a downtown LA condo. Mr. Jim respectfully declined. "I want to be with the people," he said. "I want to live here at the Dream Center and serve the community." A few months later Jim Bakker moved into Casa Grande, where the pastors were housed. Pastor Matthew gave up his personal room so Mr. Jim could have a place to live. His room was next to my room, and Pastor Tommy asked me to look after him.

A few days into Mr. Jim settling into his new life at the Dream Center, I noticed he wasn't coming around. No one had seen or heard from him. I asked the head of security and his wife, who lived in the same building, if they had seen or heard from him. They hadn't. This was strange to me, but then again, maybe he just didn't want to be bothered.

On the first day I noticed Mr. Jim had not joined us for breakfast, lunch, or dinner, I had gone through my daily routine, helping around the Dream Center, and for some reason I thought about Mr. Jim all day. So at the end of the day, I went and checked on him. I knocked on his door several times before he asked who was there. "It's me, Mr. Jim. Mondo. Are you OK? Are you hungry?"

"I am OK. Thank you," Mr. Jim responded. "I just want to be left alone."

I didn't think much of it. "All right. Have a good night," I said.

The next day, the same thing happened. Mr. Jim didn't come out of his room all day. Now I began to worry. "This isn't normal," I thought. "Maybe famous people are like that." I went back that evening to check on him again. I knocked on his door several times, and he eventually asked who was there. "It's me, Mr. Jim. Mondo. Just checking on you. Are you hungry?"

"No, I am OK. Thank you." And then he was silent.

I went back to my room and continued to read the book

Mr. Jim had given me about his life. I was amazed by what he had built and also felt heartbroken by what he had gone through. I couldn't fully understand all he had experienced and why he had become so hated by so many. I knew people in the streets who had done far worse and got less time in prison than what he described in his book. I felt compassion for him, and although I did not know him, I began to think about my father. I thought if Mr. Jim were my father needing help, what would I do? I came up with a plan.

The next day, I was on a mission. I went down to get breakfast and saw that Mr. Jim did not come down again. After I finished eating, I borrowed the knife I used to eat with and made my way to Casa Grande. I walked up the stairs, and this time I did not knock. I risked everything by picking the lock to Mr. Jim's room. If I got caught doing this, I would probably be kicked out of the Dream Center. But what kept going through my mind was that Pastor Tommy had told me to look after Mr. Jim and take care of him. That's what I was doing in my way.

I slowly picked the lock and popped open the door. Walking into a completely dark room, I was hit by the feeling of depression and loneliness in the room. The curtains covered the beautiful LA sunlight. I noticed Mr. Jim had the covers over his head, and he did not hear me come in because the TV was on loud playing the news. I walked over to the curtains and pulled them back to allow the sunlight to come in, and Jim was startled. "Why are you here?" he said. "Who let you in? Please leave me alone. I just want to be left alone."

"Mr. Jim, good morning. Why are you here all alone, man, in the dark? You haven't eaten anything since you arrived. No one deserves to be alone. This isn't right, man. Listen, Mr. Jim, I read your book, and from what I read, you are not into sports, but you do like building and shopping and good food. You are in LA, baby. We have it all. This is what we are going to do. You are going to take a bath because in your book you mentioned you like baths." I turned the bath water on, and I said, "I will be back in forty-five minutes to get you."

While I was saying this, Mr. Jim was looking at me with no emotion on his face. "If when I'm back you haven't gotten in the bath, then I am going to carry you as if you were my father, and I will put you in the bath. But I don't want to do that because you are a grown man and I know you can do it."

Then all of a sudden, a slight smile broke out on his face. "Oh!" I said. "You can smile. We will go out to eat and shop in Chinatown. I have a friend who is the contractor for the new Union Station downtown. I want you to see, and maybe you can give him some tips on how to build it."

Mr. Jim was ready in thirty minutes. We left the dark, depressed room and spent the whole day together. He was quiet for most of the time, but I could tell he was having a great time.

In the coming weeks Mr. Jim and I talked for hours. I would ask him questions about his life and what he went through. I asked him about his family, Tammy Faye, Jamie, and Tammy Sue; how he built Heritage USA and the PTL Network to reach a worldwide audience; and what it was like meeting the presidents of the United States. I also asked him about Jerry Falwell, Jessica Hahn, and why no one came to his defense. I was amazed that Mr. Jim was honest and open about the mistakes he had made. He never once defended himself to me. He took full responsibility for it all.

"Now that's gangster," I said. "You never snitched on anyone. That's more than some dudes in the streets would ever do."

I asked him how he ended up getting a forty-five-year sentence. Mr. Jim said it all came down to various people who planned his destruction. He also told me a large federal agency had framed him by getting videos of his own programs and editing them to make him say things he never said, which was one of the reasons he ended up getting accused and sentenced. Attorney Alan Dershowitz took on his appeals case and argued that the previous judge was prejudiced against him. As a result, Jim's forty-five-year sentence was overturned, and he was released on parole after serving nearly five years. Jim said that in a later civil trial he provided evidence of the videos the federal agency had altered and played them back unedited and in context. That time, he said, the jury ruled in his favor.

The news did not report that as they did in the first trial. Mr. Jim said, "The damage was already done. I lost my family; the ministry was stolen; my friends walked away; my reputation was ruined in front of the world. I lost it all. But I never lost hope in Jesus. He never left me and never forsook me. I grew closer to Him, and the reason I am still here is because I learned to forgive myself and forgave all the people who hurt me and my family from my heart." Then Mr. Jim added, "Never give up, Mondo. Never give up on God. He never gives up on you. Stay humble. I had to learn the hard way. You don't if you just walk in humility."

Mr. Jim and I began to hang out every day. He started serving the community and getting to know the people. Mr. Jim was there every Saturday for the outreach called Adopt a Block. He would pick up trash, sweep the streets, and paint the homes. At the end of the block, he prayed for the people. During the week, Mr. Jim spent his time fixing up different rooms and even helping renovate a small theater with fresh paint, carpets, picture frames, and new furniture. Mr. Jim even was approached by a well-known paint company to donate hundreds of dollars' worth of paint and brushes to update the exterior of several buildings at the Dream Center. Mr. Jim said he felt alive serving the people in the community.

One day the Dream Center was buzzing, and word got out that a very well-known athlete wanted to stop by and tour the facility. But it wasn't just any well-known athlete; it was one of the best cornerbacks in the NFL at the time. That incredible athlete spoke into my life during the tour. Pastor Tommy Barnett had asked me to share my story, and as I began to speak, I dropped my head, remembering some of the things I'd done.

Later, that NFL star stopped me and said, "Pick your head up; there is nothing to be ashamed of. God picked you and chose you. Never share your story with your head down. You are important." Then he hugged me and said, "I love you, kid. You are going to be great and do great things in your life." During the tour he asked to see Jim Bakker. He said the reverend had a word for him. Everyone around was shocked that this famous athlete would ask for Jim Bakker, let alone that Mr. Jim had a word from God for him. I walked to get Mr. Jim and told him that a famous football player was here to see him and was saying that he had a word from God to give him. As Mr. Jim got ready to go down to see him, he was praying that God would give him the word the football star was talking about. Others were in the room, and I witnessed it, and Mr. Jim and the NFL player met in the living room of Casa Grande. They greeted each other with a hug, and quickly he asked Mr. Jim to share the word that God had for him. Mr. Jim paused for a second and responded by saying, "Don't sell the farm." This was an odd word to give someone. I was thinking, "Oh no, Mr. Jim made a mistake." The room stood silent. We all watched these two legends standing facing each other, and you could hear a pin drop. Suddenly, the NFL star broke into a dance and yelled, "Yes! Yes! Yes! That's the word God had spoken to me about, 'Don't sell the farm.'" He turned to his team and said, "I told you that's the word God gave me." It was confirmation that the word he had received was right on. Mr. Jim then proceeded to explain why he should not sell the farm. This was a reminder to me about how prophetic words were given to my mother and my sister that changed my life.

Today, that football legend is still doing great things, changing lives and inspiring our culture with the gifts and calling God gave him.

Mr. Jim started to teach Bible studies each day at noon that focused on Jesus and the Book of Revelation. Hundreds of people, young and old, attended, and Mr. Jim provided lunch for everyone who came. I began to get more involved in Mr. Jim's ministry. I felt I had found a place where I fit, because Mr. Jim also had been rejected by society. Yet here he was doing whatever it took to help hurting people. One day Mr. Jim called me his "road dog," which is a compliment in prison and street culture. It meant he trusted me, that I was his best friend and right-hand man. I assisted Mr. Jim by driving him around Los Angeles, and we spent a lot of time together.

This was the start of not only a friendship but a father-and-son relationship that has continued to this day. As close as we are, we don't hold the same exact political views, and we are from different backgrounds and generations. So many people want to see that as a negative thing, but when you are family and have unconditional love for one another, you can have differences of opinion without allowing that to come between you. This is what has kept our relationship strong. Today Jim and Lori Bakker consider me one of their sons.

At the Dream Center I was on another mission for Mr. Jim. In my heart I had been praying that God would send him a companion. I tried to introduce him to different women at the church, but they weren't the right fit. One day a beautiful woman named Lori Graham was invited to speak to the women in the discipleship program to share her story of redemption. Mr. Jim was introduced to her at that event.

Ms. Lori was from Phoenix and had been working at Pastor Tommy's church there. The moment Mr. Jim saw Ms. Lori, he said he knew she was the one. Ms. Lori was exactly what Mr. Jim had been praying for in a wife. After a few days I knew Mr. Jim was head over heels for her. Even in group settings they spent most of the time talking to each other. I went out of my way to let Ms. Lori know Mr. Jim had fallen in love with her. She was shocked, but she had strong feelings for him as well. They began to date, and within seven weeks Mr. Jim and Ms. Lori were married in the Burbank mountains at the home of John and Joyce Caruso, two of the most amazing people I have ever met. They are Jim and Lori's best friends, and they have become like family to me as well.

Eventually Mr. Jim's time at the Dream Center came to an end, and he knew it was time for him to move on. He felt being around the wonderful people in the community was part of his healing process. Mr. Jim is a visionary with big dreams, and he had a vision to once again pursue what God had called him to do, which was to minister through Christian television.

Mr. Jim asked me to join his ministry and go with them back to Charlotte, North Carolina, the very place he once led

PTL and had since been mocked and ridiculed. This was an extremely difficult decision for me to make. The thought of leaving my mother, my sister, and the place that welcomed me, Los Angeles, was daunting. It's all I had known. It's who I was. It was my comfort zone, my identity. How could I walk away?

When I made my decision, I visited my mother and asked for her blessing. I knew God had opened this door for me. I wasn't looking for a free ride. All I ever wanted was someone to give me an opportunity, and perhaps this was it. I took the step of faith, not knowing what was on the other side, and walked into what would become my future.

Learning to Trust

OVER THE NEXT twenty years, Mr. Jim and I would become inseparable. He would take me under his wing and mentor me, and I would become a support beam in his life. I would come alongside him as God slowly called him back into television ministry. Together we would move ministry locations from North Carolina to Florida before ultimately settling in Branson, Missouri, our current base.

In Florida, Mr. Jim and Ms. Lori opened Camp of Hope, a place for leaders to be restored as well as a food outreach for the community. Ms. Lori had been helping a family for a decade from the inner city of Phoenix. The mother did not want the kids to end up in gangs, or worse. She and the kids ultimately traveled to Florida, where Mr. Jim and Ms. Lori had provided a home for them. The kids ended up staying with Mr. Jim and Ms. Lori. In an instant they became parents of nine children, who all lived with them in their three-bedroom home. In time, three would return to Phoenix, and one would be adopted, but the other five remained with Jim and Lori.

We all became a family. Mr. Jim and Ms. Lori became more than friends to me; they were a mom and dad. They began to look after me, and Ms. Lori would give me advice and share wisdom to help me understand what ministry life is like. She became a shoulder for me to lean on. She and Mr. Jim treated me like a son, which was a great honor for me.

The kids also had a special place in my life. Without them even knowing it, they were helping my heart heal because I saw a lot of myself in them. I also understood the pain of abandonment. As the kids settled into their new life with Mr. Jim and Ms. Lori, it was just natural that I would fall into the role of big brother. I could see that the kids needed someone familiar, someone who understood their culture. Because I could relate, I was able to help Mr. Jim and Ms. Lori understand how the kids were feeling and thinking. There were times when Mr. Jim and Ms. Lori had difficulties disciplining them because culturally the kids would not respond to them. They would almost gang up on Mr. Jim and Ms. Lori. I would be called on to step in and help.

I understood these kids; I knew where they were coming from. I gained their trust, and we have built our relationship on that trust over the last two decades. They are my brother and sisters. People say blood is thicker than water, but that isn't always true. My love for Maricela, Lori, Clarissa, Ricky, Marie, Sergio, Paul, Adriana, and Jenny knows no difference. They are my family. We understand each other, and we protect each other fiercely, but like all families, we aren't perfect. We are all different with different views on life. But at the end of the day, we love one another. They have given me the greatest gift they can: a place in their life. They all have grown into beautiful people, creating their own families. I am beyond proud of them.

Completing the family was Ms. Lori's mom, Grandma Char. She was one of the most amazing ladies I have ever met. Loving, kind, and compassionate, she became a grandmother to all of us. Her wisdom, guidance, and prayers gave us the courage to believe in ourselves. She became the heart of the ministry. She graduated into heaven in 2021 and is greatly missed every single day.

While in Florida the ministry was housed on borrowed land, and the owners had other plans than for a ministry to be built on it. Wanting to find a more permanent location, Mr. Jim and Ms. Lori decided to make a move to middle America. By this time other staff had joined the team, and when Mr. Jim and Ms. Lori were offered an opportunity in Branson, Missouri, we all packed up and headed to the Midwest. I had no idea where Branson was, but when we arrived, we were welcomed by a wonderful community of people.

Branson had a reputation for being a musical town, and we got to know some amazing musicians, including singers Tony Orlando and Andy Williams and the bluegrass/country rock band The Dillards. They all embraced us with open arms. The late Gary Smalley, a respected family counselor who lived in Branson, and a large number of the local pastors also made us feel at home. Branson is a beautiful place with beautiful people. It felt as if we were living in *The Andy Griffith Show*. But it wasn't a television set; this was our new home.

When we arrived, Branson developers Jerry and Dee Crawford provided a home for us and the ministry. The Crawford family was deeply touched by Mr. Jim's ministry back during the days of Heritage USA, and they wanted to do something special for us to give us a new start. Jerry believed in Jim and the call on his life, so Jerry bought an old Cowboy Cafe restaurant, and he and Mr. Jim started making plans to turn it into a TV studio. Against all odds, we launched what is now called *The Jim Bakker Show* in 2003. We will be forever grateful for Jerry and Dee and their beautiful family.

———◆———

As Mr. Jim relaunched his television ministry, we also started building what is now known as Morningside USA, the home of *The Jim Bakker Show*. I would learn television production, camera operation, lighting direction, television direction, and the proper way to conduct an interview. Eventually I would cohost *The Jim Bakker Show* with Jim and then produce my own program, *The Mondo Show*. Remember when I was just a young boy in Central America dreaming of hosting my own television show? Where did that desire come from, especially since I had little exposure to it. Well, here I am, producing television shows.

The moment I met Mr. Jim, a mentoring process began that has changed my life. A good mentor will always challenge you to be the best but also allow you to finish your own race to go to the next level. A great mentor will allow you to make mistakes but not leave you alone in those mistakes. A good mentor doesn't have to speak to impact you. A good mentor will always challenge you to carry yourself better and make wise decisions. But you have to be willing to go through real-life struggles in order to see a change.

I was still in the process of surrendering many areas of my life. Undoing the mindset of the street takes time. God was still working in me, and He used Mr. Jim and other mentors to help me grow. Lasting change happens when you work and walk alongside your mentor. The mentor has to allow you to see their good, their bad, their ugly, their downfalls, their dark side, and their triumphs. The problem is most people only see their mentors at their best; they only see them after they write a book or speak before a big crowd. Seeing the mentor behind the curtain is what will help you grow. But very few mentors are willing to be that vulnerable. This is why we have a hurting generation in the church, because they never see leaders behind the mask. Most mentors don't allow you to see their struggles. Jim allowed me to see his process, and I am forever grateful.

Good mentors also walk with you through the process of conviction. To me, conviction is what changes everything. It reveals what you have to tear out of your life in order to rebuild on a firm foundation. Conviction is attached to change. Most people don't want to let go of the old because we're scared to change.

In 2020, after Mr. Jim went through some health challenges, including a stroke, he asked me to cohost the show alongside Ms. Lori while he was out of commission. "I want you, Maricela, and Little Lori to help host my show without me," he said.

This was probably one of the most fulfilling yet scariest times of my life. Mr. Jim was entrusting me with his national television program, watched by millions of people. He could have called some of the greatest Christian leaders in the world to come in and cohost the show. Yet he reached out to me for help. God had reserved that moment for me. He had been preparing me for years, working in my life; I just hadn't grasped it completely.

I started *The Mondo Show* in 2019. Jim trusted me when I told him God had put in my heart to start my own show. *The Mondo Show* is distributed across America and around the world on the PTL Network. It currently has millions of viewers each month and is growing.

In the last twenty-something years, I've learned keys that make you a good television host. What an unexpected turn of events, to go from the streets to interviewing the greatest Christian leaders of our time. I may seem very different from the people I interview, but what we have in common is the gospel and a heart for hurting people.

By being faithful to my simple assignment to drive people around, I was placed in the right spot at the right time. All this time I was being prepared. I know God called me, but I have to choose to do the work and meet Him halfway. With hard work and dedication, I began to see the results. I had prepared for this moment, and I was now ready to step into it.

I had read books about television production and spent hours after work lighting the sets, trying different camera positions, and learning how to produce and direct TV shows. I pestered former directors and producers with questions, and I watched other interview shows, paying special attention to how the hosts connected with the audience. Jim Bakker also shared his insights with me. On top of all that, I read books on a variety of subjects, such as history and politics; I also studied the Bible in Greek and Hebrew, and earned degrees in theology and art. When others went out to dinner and a movie with friends, I stayed back and worked on my craft. I was focused and driven to be the best. I worked on my delivery, presentation, and interviewing skills, and when my time came, I was ready.

I once thought my past actions disqualified me, but God orchestrated my steps to bring me where I am today. God is bigger than you or me. He exists outside time and sees the end and the beginning. When I was a little boy, even when I was in the gangs, people said I was different. I survived because God's hand protected me.

When I stop and think about the mentors God brought into my life, I'm amazed. Pastors Tommy and Matthew Barnett came into my life and believed in me. When Pastor Tommy and Pastor Matthew gave me the opportunity, I spent time with them and talked to them. They encouraged me. I wanted to keep serving people partly because they were serving people. I was far from perfect, but they still loved me. They gave me hope. They gave me the foundation I needed.

Then Jim Bakker came into my life. Mr. Jim is more than a mentor; he is a father. Mr. Jim taught me to realize that no matter what happens, God will never leave me or forsake me—never.

One thing about Mr. Jim is that he has always been transparent with me. He never sugarcoated or hid anything. He allowed me to see behind the scenes into what he went through. When I started serving with him in ministry, I got to see Mr. Jim when no one else was watching. I saw how he prayed, how he read the Bible. I saw how he dealt with rejection. I saw how he dealt with people not liking him and how he was able to forgive people. I learned from Jim Bakker that you trust God, learn to hear from God, stay humble, and forgive those who hurt you.

Another man who came into my life is one of the greatest theologians in the Christian world: R. T. Kendall, who has written hundreds of books and was pastor of Westminster Chapel in London for twenty-five years. Imagine him hooking up with a gangster like me. He came into my life and began to pour into me and teach me about forgiveness. I had a lot of unforgiveness in my heart due to my past. I still had so much anger inside me, but God brought R. T. Kendall into my life at the right time.

We became friends. We would call each other, and he would come visit. Mr. Jim had been touched by his writings when he was in prison. And when Jim Bakker invited R. T. into his life after prison, I had the privilege of befriending R. T. in a way I never imagined. I would sit for hours and talk with him about my life. He would call and email and just check on me. My life was changed by his mentoring.

Another mentor is Rick Joyner, an incredible author and the founder of MorningStar Ministries. He provided a home for Mr. Jim and Ms. Lori and me, as well as the ministry, when we moved to North Carolina. It was during that time that I developed a friendship with Rick. He provided me with a car so I could go to his Bible school. I had never thought in a million years that I would ever get to meet, let alone be around, Rick Joyner. While at the Dream Center I was given a copy of his book *The Final Quest*, and it touched me deeply. I had no idea that one day I would call him a friend.

Gary Smalley, who was one of the greatest relationship counselors in the world, came into my life when we moved to Branson, Missouri. He and his wife, Norma, invited Mr.

Jim and Ms. Lori and all us kids to their home for dinner. He became a frequent guest on *The Jim Bakker Show*, and Gary and I struck up a fast friendship. He began to teach me how to heal from past relationships and treat people with kindness and unconditional love. I never wanted to get married, but God brought Gary into my life for a season to prepare me for marriage. Gary used to say the only thing we will take into heaven is relationships. With his words Gary changed my outlook and gave me hope that one day I could be married. Gary and I would talk almost every week. No matter where he was in the world, he would call me, and when he was in town, we would go to dinner. Gary Smalley loved me unconditionally. In many ways he saved my life.

Another great man God placed in my life two years ago was someone I had the honor of interviewing on *The Mondo Show*: baseball legend Darryl Strawberry. He helped lead the New York Mets to a World Series championship in 1986 and the New York Yankees in 1996, 1998, and 1999. I was a huge LA Dodgers fan growing up, and Darryl Strawberry was my favorite player. I'm not going to tell his story, but after going through years and years of struggles, he has become the definition of redemption.

Darryl and I both love Jesus, and I am so grateful God has restored him. Today, I consider him a Crenshaw brother, since he's also from Los Angeles. I have so much love for him for never giving up. I still can't believe we are friends. We both should have been dead long ago, but God had other plans for us.

Through so many relationships God has taught me to trust Him more and to trust His plans. I had no idea, but someone was about to walk into my world and catch my attention in a way I did not expect. My whole life was about to change.

Chapter 19

"Who's That Girl?"

WHEN YOU WATCH a person jump in the trenches of life with you, getting in the mud with you, coming through for you again and again, your love for that person shoots off the charts. That's my wife, Elizabeth. I call her Liz. This chapter is our story. It's another amazing and undeniably miraculous account of God guiding my circumstances to my future of becoming an honorable man, husband, and father.

I must say that no one has been a greater mentor in my life than my wife. More than anything, she has taught me how to love and how to better understand myself. She has taught me what it means to be a real man, not what my homies in the gangs taught me and not the images my father left imprinted on my mind. Without her even knowing, Liz shows me that love doesn't give up. I've learned greatly from all the mentors God has put in my life, but with Liz, I am walking it out in real time, 24/7.

She sees the good, the bad, and the ugly in me like no one

else does. Yet she knows my heart, believes in me, sees my potential, and embraces my calling. Liz has an unreal amount of grace for me. But before we can move on, we surprisingly need to go all the way back to the night I had been brutally beaten by the police and dropped off into the Bloods' neighborhood. I bet you didn't see that one coming.

Before those cops took us into the alley to beat us and then drop us in enemy territory, they took us to the police station to interrogate us. They didn't book us on anything, but we were in handcuffs, waiting in a holding cell. There were some other gang members being held with us, and we were being questioned about a crime that had taken place. Nobody was talking, though, which was infuriating the police. That could have added to our beating in the alley later. But we'd been trained not to say anything. It was either get punished by the police if you didn't talk or by the streets if you did.

We were left sitting in the cell for several hours, not knowing what they were going to do to us. Interestingly the radio was playing in the background, and Dick Clark's voice came on. He said that for the next hour we'd have the Lennon Sisters, and they would be sharing stories and singing songs from their living room. This was the first time I'd ever heard of the Lennon Sisters. I didn't know who they were. For decades, beginning in the mid-1950s, they were America's sweethearts. From 1955 to 1968 the group appeared regularly on *The Lawrence Welk Show* before having their own television show. Through the years, they were regulars on many television shows and had numerous hit songs. The Lennon Sisters are part of the legacy of America. In 1987 they received a star on the Hollywood Walk of Fame. In 2001 they were inducted into the Vocal Group Hall of Fame, and in 2022 they received the New Standard Award from the Great American Songbook Foundation.

At first, I was thinking, "This is the last thing I want to hear!" Yet as the hour went by, I was moved by their warm, beautiful voices as the sisters sang Christmas songs, played guitars and the piano with their other siblings, and shared family stories, all from their living room. You could feel the joy and love coming through the airwaves. It was as if time had stopped and I was transported to *that* living room, singing and experiencing *that* family atmosphere. The last time I remembered having fun with family was in Central America when we shot firecrackers, exchanged gifts, and had a feast. Relatives from all over came to celebrate.

But those good times were such a faded memory, it was almost as if they never happened. In that police station I felt lonely and empty, as if I wasn't valued. I felt as though no one cared anymore. I constantly was being told, "See, you guys are nothing. You guys are worthless. No one's thinking about you." And I was thinking, "I wonder what it would be like to be in the Lennon Sisters' living room." The music playing on the radio was my escape from thinking about what the police were going to do to us.

Visualizing my life in the family of the Lennon Sisters was more than a passing thought. It was an unusual moment in time for me that years later would be a signpost I could look back on as another evidence of God directing my life.

Now, fast-forward from that moment in the holding cell almost two decades later. I had come out of the abuse of Central America, the street gangs of Los Angeles, and the Dream Center season, and now was in Branson. What you need to grasp here is that I'm a Latino former gangster from inner-city LA, and Branson is the polar opposite. Nothing is wrong with that; it's just the exact opposite of where I came from, and that is significant to this story.

By this time I was in charge of producing and directing *The Jim Bakker Show*. My job involved setting up and lighting the set, directing and producing the program, and working with the live audience to ensure everyone was seated in the best location for the broadcast. This particular day, I was moving people to certain spots for the best camera angles and the right background when this stunning young woman walked in. Stunning is an understatement. She was the most beautiful woman I'd ever seen. Everyone on the production team and in the audience paused to take note of her beauty. She wasn't showy or loud but radiant and confident. She carried herself with so much dignity and value it was as if every step she took were in slow motion. And I thought, "Who is that girl? What's her name?"

She sat down in the studio audience next to someone I also knew. Unbeknownst to me, this friend had wanted Elizabeth and me to meet almost four years before. "Beth," she said, "you've got to come and meet this guy who is working at the studio. He's perfect for you."

I moved them and the tables around several times just because I wanted to get a closer look at her and make sure my eyes were not playing tricks on me, that she was actually as beautiful as she appeared when she first walked in the door. While moving them around, I got another shock when she spoke to me and said, *"Jefe, no quisiera tener que moverlas otra vez."* ("Boss, I don't want to be moved one more time.") I was in shock not because of what she said but because she spoke to me in Spanish, my first language.

Again, this is Branson, Missouri. I had been living with Jim and Lori Bakker and their family. I had been away from Los Angeles for a long time and had not heard Spanish in years. Spanish is not what you speak in this town. So when she spoke to me in Spanish, she got my attention, and it caught my heart. I began to talk to her and asked, "What is your name?"

"Elizabeth," she said.

I said, "No, I don't like that name. What else do they call you?"

"They call me Beth."

I said, "No, I don't like that either. I'm going to call you Liz." A real charmer, right? What a way to make an impression. It was the most foolish, arrogant thing to do. I asked her if she could stay afterward to talk. Amazingly she agreed!

After the program we began to talk, and the more we talked, the more captivated I became. We instantly had a connection. She was different from any other girl that I had met to that day. She was intelligent. She knew about politics. She had been born and raised in Venice, California, which is a Los Angeles neighborhood. She knew the culture I had come from and the culture I understood. She knew the music I listened to. She knew the language I was speaking. And she knew the Lord. She is a strong Catholic.

We talked for hours at Studio City Café, where we recorded the show at that time, and I asked if I could meet her later that night. We met at IHOP and ended up talking all night long. We shared our hopes and dreams and also our pain. I had never opened up with anyone like that before. We told each other our deepest, darkest secrets and the most intimate moments of our pasts. She shared some of the most wonderful moments in her life as well as some of the most difficult. She thought she was going to scare me off or that I was going to be shocked. But all I felt toward her was compassion and love, something I had never experienced with anyone.

I did not want that night to end. I just wanted to be around her because there was something about her that I had never experienced. It changed my life. I had been dating someone else for four years, and the day after that first night speaking with Liz, I met up with the girl I had been dating and broke up with her. Then Liz and I started dating.

This is so funny but again shows my juvenile behavior at the time. When we were at IHOP, I emphatically laid out to Liz that there were three things I was *never* going to do. "One, I'm never getting married. Two, I'm never going to marry a Mexican girl. Three, I'm never going to have kids." She just looked back at me with her deep hazel eyes and, without flinching, replied, "Well, that's too bad for you because I'm getting married. I'm a Mexican American girl. And I am having kids. We'll see what happens." The way she responded drew me to her even more. I loved her realness. She wasn't trying to win me over or fit in with me.

———◦———

Here's where the story begins to get pretty miraculous. By this time, Gary Smalley and I had struck up a friendship that turned into him becoming a regular guest on the show. He had been mentoring me and teaching me marriage principles, even though I told him I was never getting married. Well, he was also counseling Liz and had been for years, even when she was living in California. Liz had gone through a horrible time with addiction and other serious trauma. She did a year in outpatient drug rehab. That was something we discussed on our first date. We just got everything out there. When Liz was going through her drug issues, Gary flew out to California and helped save her life. When she completed rehab, she moved to Branson, where Gary met with her weekly.

One thing about me is I am real. I don't sugarcoat or put on a religious mask. Instead of getting married, Liz and I moved in together. We even bought and remodeled a house together. We justified playing house—at least I did. Honestly I tried not to think about whether what we were doing was right or wrong. Deep down, however, we knew it was not God's plan. I was still resisting marriage due to what I'd seen in my past. I'm not excusing myself; I'm just grateful that God's grace was bigger. Though we were out of His will, He was moving in Liz's life.

The Holy Spirit was convicting Liz. One morning after we'd been dating for two years, Liz came to me and said, "Mondo, I am not upset with you. I understand. I love you, and I get that you never want to get married. And that's OK. I wish it was you. I feel in my heart like I'm meant to be with you. But I cannot choose you over God one more day. And until you decide to honor me as your wife, I'm gone." Liz packed up her stuff, and through her tears she left. I was devastated, but it was the wake-up call I needed.

I did not waste time. I called my mother and said, "Mom, I need to talk to you. The girl of my dreams, the girl I feel I need to spend the rest of my life with, just walked away from me and the home we built. I need to know why I'm not able to step out and marry her. Why am I so scared to have children? Why am I afraid?"

And then I asked my mother a question that I was afraid to ask but needed to ask: "What happened to my dad and you?

What happened to your marriage? Because whatever happened to you and Dad is what's keeping me from being in a committed marriage." I told her, "I want to surrender my life fully to God. I want this area of my life to be made right with God, and I need your help, Mom. Please, tell me what happened, because this will determine whether I go after Liz or I let her go just like I have done in the past."

My mother began to give me wisdom. She told me that her mistakes were not going to be my mistakes, that the mistakes she and my father made in their relationship were not mine. She told me God had cleared my life of their mistakes. My mom began to pour wisdom into me and give me hope. She began to tell me that God had called me to be a good man and a great husband, that God had prepared me and had given me the wisdom to be a father one day. My mother's words gave me the courage to not let Liz go but to go after her and ask her parents for her hand in marriage.

After a few hours I hung up the phone and fell to my knees. I asked God to forgive me for manipulating this area in my life. I asked Him to forgive me for my arrogance and for thinking that as long as I served in ministry and helped people, He would be OK with me not surrendering that area of my life. I began to cry from the depth of my soul for thinking I could make a deal with Him; it was a cry so deep inside my soul and spirit that I can't explain it. As I was weeping, I was letting go of the soul ties and the pain of the past.

If my life was going to change, I had to go all in. When I finished pouring out my soul to the Lord, I wiped my tears away and cleaned myself up. But I prayed about this for four days. Then I called Liz's parents and asked if I could meet with them. They granted me the opportunity to meet. I'd tried calling Liz over those four days, but she was holding strong, boy! She would not answer my calls. So I texted her and said I was going to meet with her parents and ask them if I could marry her. She simply replied, "OK. You may call me after."

Liz's parents are two of the kindest, most understanding people I have ever met. Her mother, Mimi, comes from a big Catholic, Irish/Mexican family. She is one of twelve children all born to the same parents. The importance of family is deeply ingrained in them. Mimi was always welcoming, and she seemed to look past everything that had happened in my past and not hold it against me. All she wanted was her daughter's happiness, and if I could treat her better and love her more than anyone else would, that was her greatest desire.

Liz's father, Danny, comes from a big family as well. He is one of eight children from a beautiful Catholic family. Danny has played a pivotal role in my life. Danny is Mexican American. When I met him, I was extremely nervous. In my life, I haven't had the greatest relationships with Hispanic men. To be completely honest, I had never had a deep, healthy relationship with one. But Danny was different. He is strong yet gentle. He would listen to me and not judge me. He would always greet me with a handshake and a hug. Can you imagine that? I had always been uncomfortable when people would try to hug me, but he was comforting. He was safe. That may be because he comes from a family that values genuinely loving one another. Liz's parents and their families were a huge reason I thought maybe marriage and family could be in my future.

I went to their home, and we sat down in their kitchen and began to talk. I told them I was in love with their daughter, and I asked them to forgive me for hurting them. I had hurt them and their daughter by not being man enough to approach our relationship the right way. I needed their blessing. I wanted them to know their daughter had changed my life and that I wanted to be a part of her life. I wanted to be a good husband. They gave me their blessing, and as soon as they did, I began to plan how I was going to propose.

I decided to propose on April 18, 2009. We had gone ring shopping earlier that week, and she chose a small but beautiful ring. Liz is all about modesty and simple beauty, but she was being very humble about which ring she selected. I told the jeweler to put it away and I'd come back and get it. But a few days later I went back and asked him to show me the biggest ring he had, and I bought it that day. It was the most beautiful ring I'd ever seen. With the ring in hand, I made up my mind that I was going to propose that night.

I took her to the lake and brought a blanket. The sun was going down, and the sunset was beautiful. I parked my car and put on some romantic music. I made a fire and sat with her on the blanket. I began to tell her how I felt. "I don't know what it is to be a husband, but when I found you, you changed my life," I said. "I know God brought you to me. You have been an angel in my life. I love you and want to spend the rest of my life with you.

"Liz," I said, "my life has been rough, but they say in every rough there is a diamond."

The sun had dropped below the horizon, and there was no light other than the fire. I got down on one knee and asked Elizabeth to be my wife. I placed the ring on her finger, and she began to cry because, as she put it, all she wanted was me. She hugged me, and we cried together and celebrated.

On October 3, 2009, Gary Smalley officiated our wedding ceremony. As I stood at the altar, waiting for my bride to walk down the aisle, so many thoughts came into my mind. I never imagined this day would come for me, and yet there I was. The church was filled with family and friends who heard me say over and over again, "I am never going to get married." But the moment the church doors open and I saw Liz walk toward me, it all made sense. God brought her into my life to change me.

When we became husband and wife, it was one of the best moments of my life. We headed off to the reception with two hundred guests in tow. After our first dance as man and wife, my new father-in-law gave a toast. As he was finishing the toast, without him knowing it, he said the exact words I had heard in that old Spanish church. He looked at me and said, "Mondo, welcome home." Being married to Liz just felt right. I knew I was home.

Two months later we were preparing to spend our first Christmas together as a married couple. December 21 is a night I'll never forget. Liz's relatives started arriving at our home, one family at a time. Her family is unlike any I have ever met. Their Christmas parties are like something out of a Hollywood movie. Everyone is happy and so loving. Because her mom is one of twelve, there are thirty-plus cousins. You would think it would be a bit chaotic, but it's just the opposite. It's perfection.

Now, remember back to that day when I was in a holding cell and my only comfort was the Lennon Sisters' hour. I had spent so much time envisioning what it would be like to spend time with a family like that. As crazy miraculous as it sounds, I didn't have to envision it anymore. My wife is the daughter of Mimi Lennon, one of the Lennon Sisters. Here they were, in my house. The family was together, singing and telling stories.

Just hearing their angelic voices brought tears to my eyes. Still to this day I can't believe it. Only God could do that, man. Only God.

Chapter 20

The Necklace

THROUGHOUT MY LIFE I have received those dreaded phone calls informing me that a close friend or family member had passed away. I've had homeboys die in my arms from drive-bys or fights that went wrong. Death had surrounded me on the streets, but nothing prepared me for the phone call I received on May 31, 2009. It felt as if I'd been sucker punched in the gut as the person on the other end of the phone cried and sobbed out the news. My father had been murdered, shot down in front of his home, the same home I had lived in as a little boy.

A few weeks before that Liz and I had gotten engaged. We celebrated with family and friends, and one of the people I called to share the good news with was my father. Years earlier, after my grandfather passed away, my mother traveled to Central America for the funeral, and during that trip my father met with her and asked her forgiveness. The two talked for hours and were able to make peace. He wanted to see my sister and me, and at the end of that year, we traveled to Central America to meet him.

I was still in the gang, still filled with hurt and anger, and my plan was to get even with him. All I really wanted was for my father to hug me and tell me he loved me and why he didn't stay with us, why he didn't keep fighting for us, why he didn't get help to be a good husband and father. But I didn't have the tools to communicate that to him. So instead, I put a pistol in his face.

He didn't get mad; he just looked back at me and said, "Go ahead, pull the trigger; I deserve it." I lowered the gun but was too hurt and wounded to form any kind of relationship at that time. When I made it back to Los Angeles, I tried to put him out of my mind. Over the years, however, my father would continue to seek to be a part of my life and my sister's, even if it was from a distance. In time, my heart toward him began to soften a bit, and we began working on developing some sort of relationship. We hadn't had the best of interactions, but we communicated and were respectful to each other. There just had been so much pain it prevented me from getting too close. And the distance only added to my detachment. Plus, throw in the fact that we were both opinionated and strong-willed, and you can see why it was a recipe for failure.

Surprisingly, though, my father was becoming kinder and more loving. He had many regrets. He started telling me that he loved me and was proud of me. He expressed how sorry he was for not being there for me. It seemed that just about every time we spoke over the phone, he would tell me how ashamed he felt about what had happened between him and my mother. He was embarrassed and would ask me for forgiveness. Again and again, I told him, "Dad, you don't have to keep asking for forgiveness. I am forgiving you. It's OK. Life goes on."

Still, emotionally we were not able to have a relationship the way we wished we could have. Neither of us had the tools to open up fully to each other and be vulnerable. We continued to talk, but it became more like bantering back and forth, as he passionately shared his opinion about my life choices—why I had joined the gang, why I was dating certain women, and even why I was serving in ministry, which provided little to no pay. This in turn made me defensive. That said, we made the effort to stay in touch and communicate as much as we could. Sometimes when we did try to visit, we didn't know what to say to each other, so we would just talk some on a surface level like acquaintances would. "Hi. How are you doing? Did you watch the latest *fútbol* [soccer] game with Messi?" We both loved the Argentine player Leo Messi.

In the end, however, we couldn't get beyond the hurts from the past and missed out on what could have been. So when I called my father to let him know I was getting married, I had something else I also wanted to discuss with him. I wanted him to come and be my best man. I knew it was a bold, risky request. But something inside me was hoping for healing. I thought this would be a good gesture of forgiveness. However, the conversation didn't go as I expected. I think my father was shocked. He had a lot of pent-up emotions he wanted to get out, but he didn't know how to communicate with me.

At first, he seemed amazed because in the past I'd been so adamant about never getting married and having a relationship end up like his and my mom's had. Instead of celebrating my engagement, his walls went up, and he asked me about the weather. It bothered me so much that I said, "How are you going to ask me how the weather is? Why aren't you telling me that you're happy for me?" We got into an argument, and the conversation didn't go anywhere. His response hurt me so much. I didn't know what to say, and our words to each other were too strong.

Yet I still asked him if he wanted to be my best man, and he said yes. He said he was going to work hard to get a visa to come to the United States and be a part of the wedding. He was going to do everything he could. I found out later that he and my sister had talked, and that turned him around for the better, and he wanted to try to come even more. I'm so happy for that. My sister had a way with my father that I didn't have. She just had more compassion and grace than I ever did at that time. They had a great conversation, and my sister shared with me that he was so proud of me. He was so excited. He was happy for me. He wished us the best, and he was so honored that I would even ask him to be my best man. He shared wonderful things with my sister about the conversation he and I had. Yet he also told her that he felt we couldn't connect, that he fell short.

Sadly, that was the last conversation I ever had with him. I expected him to come to my wedding and find out what my life was about here in America. I didn't expect anything to happen to him in the meantime. This was truly devastating.

When I was a young kid, my father had been my hero. He was the man I had idolized and wanted to be like. When he disappeared from my life, the running and hiding from him, the streets, time, and circumstances would change me. I was a kid who had been tossed to the wolves, forced to grow up too soon, and was trying to survive. During those critical years of my development, my father was still a man with deep unresolved issues whom we had to distance ourselves from. There was no going back to him. Because of my own anger and hate, I didn't know how to love or reach out to him, and I thought he certainly didn't love me.

I was wrong about that. I see that clearly as I look back on our fumbled attempts at reconciliation in the later years. I miss him and think about him every single day. There are times in my sleep when I will cry for my father because I miss him so much. After all the woundedness he caused me, I still loved him and had forgiven him. However, I never allowed him to occupy the place in my heart he held before he beat my mom.

Right before I got the call that my dad had been killed, I was watching a music award show and was excited because one of my favorite artists, Eminem, was making a great comeback. One second, I was smiling and joyful. Then, right in the middle of that moment, something strange happened. It was similar to the sense I had gotten in the lowrider that day before my homeboy got shot at the pay phone instead of me. This strong feeling came over me that I was going to receive a phone call that was going to change my life.

When my phone rang, it was my mother. I didn't know if I should take it or wait and call back. I decided to pick it up and heard my mother screaming through broken sobs. "What happened?" I asked. "Calm down and tell me what's going on." Before she could answer, though, I knew what had happened.

"Your father has just been murdered," she said, confirming my thoughts. "And your cousin has been murdered too," she added, her voice cracking.

Not only had I lost my father, but I also lost my cousin, who was defending my dad. You have to understand, my father always had a gun with him. As I mentioned before, he was one of the best sharpshooters in Central America. The man knew how to handle a gun. He was licensed to carry and always had a gun on him. It is part of the way of life. Central America is a very violent place. Those working in the coffee fields and as executives in that industry knew they needed to carry a weapon to defend themselves against robbers, who were always looking for a way to steal from them.

But the day my dad was shot, he wasn't carrying his gun. Just weeks before, my sister had told me he had stopped carrying. His heart had changed. He wanted peace and to not provoke anyone. He was doing everything he could to be able to come to my wedding to be my best man. But that Sunday evening, after having dinner with the family, my father and my cousins went outside to drink their coffee and smoke cigarettes. The house was on a busy main street, and there was commerce at the markets on Sundays. Crowds were on the sidewalks shopping. As my father and cousins were outside, laughing and telling stories, catching up on soccer games and the latest news, suddenly, three men with guns rushed toward my father, firing at him. My cousins were carrying guns and returned fire, but this one time, my father didn't have a gun and could not defend himself. If he had been carrying a weapon, I believe he would still be alive. He ended up making the ultimate sacrifice when he chose peace over violence.

He was gunned down in front of the home where I had been born and spent my early years. It was the same home my father grew up in, the home my grandparents had built. My cousin tried to defend my father, and he ended up being killed too. With the phone call that my dad had been murdered, it seemed as if every emotion you could imagine arose in me— anger, rage, the feeling that I needed to get revenge. I collapsed and just began to cry and cry and cry. Liz was comforting me. When Gary Smalley got word, he rushed over to be by my side. He sat and hugged me. As he held me tight, I began to shake and weep from the depths of my soul. I cried until there were no more tears.

That night, I asked God to forgive me for not being compassionate to my father. It was all I could do. I never got to say goodbye to him. Liz and I and my mother and sister flew to Central America to be part of his funeral, but by the time we arrived, it was too late. They had already buried him. When I showed up at his home—my home—it was like going back in time. I saw friends I had not seen since I was a little boy, the streets I used to run in, the playgrounds where I used to play soccer. The people in the town were in disbelief that my father had been murdered. He was killed like a dog and left on the street, his body riddled with bullets. I've often wondered what was going through my father's mind when he was struck down. What's twisted is the person who pulled the trigger was someone my father grew up with and trusted. It was someone he called family. Yet this man and his people betrayed my father and took his life with zero regard.

For a minute I thought about gathering some of my homeboys from the streets and taking revenge. But just as quickly, God touched my heart and told me I had to forgive those people. He reminded me that vengeance is His. It is not up to me to bring justice. I needed to lay down my desire for revenge and humble myself. I had to let that desire for vengeance die.

Otherwise, it would have continued to the next generation—my cousins' and my sister's kids.

Letting go of the desire to retaliate was one of the hardest things because I grew up taking revenge and settling debts. Now Christ is in me; the Word is in me. He provoked me to forgive my father's killers from the depths of my heart. That was a moment when I knew the gospel truly had penetrated my soul.

The only thing that could end the pain in my heart was to forgive from my heart—not just with my words but sincerely. That's something Jim Bakker and R. T. Kendall, two of my dear mentors, had shown me. No matter how hard it was, I had to put forgiveness into action. It would be a battle between my desires and my spirit, but I needed to trust God fully with what just took place.

The only possession I have of my father's—the only thing of his I ever wanted—is the necklace he was wearing. It is a cross with Christ on it. I have that necklace and wear it every single day. It is a remembrance that Jesus Christ has forgiven my father's killers—and He had forgiven my father. Now I can live every single day in peace because by the grace of God I have been able to forgive the people who have hurt me the most, even my father.

Chapter 21

When God Laughed

W HEN I WAS growing up, the thought of becoming a father never crossed my mind. I was scared to be a father and couldn't understand why anyone would want to bring a child into this world. The idea was beyond me. All I saw were men who made babies and then abandoned them. What kind of father could just walk away? How could a man not stay long enough to see his own seed grow?

My feelings about fatherhood were so dark and full of anger that thinking of myself as a father disgusted me. Anytime a woman I was dating talked to me seriously about having children, I became emotionally detached and often sabotaged the relationship. Conversations about bringing another life into the world messed with my mind so much that I would become physically sick. I would be transported back in time to the painful moments in my childhood that I wasn't ready to unpack. Just being around children made me anxious and claustrophobic.

Parents made me nervous too because most of the ones I

saw were letting their kids get away with bad behavior. The kids were running the show, not the parents. Even in my young, rebellious mind, I understood that children needed discipline and guidance, something I didn't get early on. With the epidemic of absentee fathers, no wonder the kids in the streets didn't know how to navigate their emotions, were out of control, and used drugs and alcohol. Many ended up in prison. Perhaps if they'd had fathers guiding them, those outcomes could have been prevented.

In every way the thought of being a father absolutely terrified me.

When I finally got married to my dream girl, Liz, I knew from day one of our dating relationship that kids were a priority. Two weeks after we got married, we decided to just go for it. She was ready to be a mother. That was her dream. My loving and generous response was, "OK, we can start trying, but you can only get pregnant once. No more." Oh, what a charmer I was.

My problem was that the fear of fatherhood and the sharp, jagged edges of my childhood were still cutting into me. I was acting out of my woundedness. What was I even thinking, telling my wife she could only get pregnant once and no more, as if I could control God's plans or my wife? I was trying to manipulate God and life itself, as if that were even possible! Someone told me years ago, "If you want to make God laugh, tell him your plans." I think God laughed the day I said, "Once and no more," because Liz got pregnant once—with twins!

When I found out we were having twins, I became undone inside and fear began to overwhelm me. As much as I tried to pretend everything was OK, I was an emotional wreck, and it affected my behavior. Liz was the steady one. My response was to become stoic and withdrawn. Unable to communicate my feelings to her, I simply pretended I was OK while the fear inside was tormenting me. I didn't want to fail her or the twins. Having children may be the most beautiful thing, but getting there was going to be a difficult journey, both for me and for Liz.

At this time I had an opportunity to begin traveling to share my story, and that would be a way for me to provide for my family. But on two separate occasions, Jim Bakker and Gary Smalley gave me the best advice. They said, "Don't go around the world trying to win the lost and lose your own family." I knew what I needed to do, and that was to stay home, be with Liz, see the kids grow up, and be part of their lives. And that's what I decided to do. God knew I would be needed at home.

At week six of the pregnancy Liz started to bleed. We were both in fear that we may lose the babies. We prayed daily for God to keep them inside her. She remained steadfast and strong. She prayed daily and spoke life into the babies all the time. She experienced a small amount of bleeding through the entire pregnancy and was on strict bed rest from week six until week twenty-two. Her parents, Mimi and Danny, stepped in and were amazing. Liz may be my wife, but she is still their baby girl.

I would drop her off at their house Monday through Friday from 8:00 a.m. to 5:30 p.m. while I went to work. She would lie down the entire day because sitting or standing would make her bleed more. Mimi and Danny made all her meals and would have dinner ready for me when I got to their house. Talk about unbelievable! I never had "parents" care for me like that. I wondered, "Is this real parenting?" They were showing me what unconditional love looked like, and I will be forever grateful to them for that.

At week twenty-two Liz and I went to her specialist. They did an ultrasound, and we both knew something was wrong by the look on the doctor's face. Liz's cervix was open from the top, and she was in labor. She was admitted to the hospital immediately. They told us that she wouldn't be leaving the hospital until she had the babies. And so the long journey began.

———◆———

Liz stayed in the hospital for seventy-two days, the rest of what proved to be an extremely rough and at times life-threatening pregnancy. We almost lost the twins. However, this led to another series of miracles that God would use to mold my heart. Three days a week I drove an hour from the ministry to see Liz at the hospital, staying overnight on the weekends. Her mom and dad were angels. Extended family members also rallied around my wife, encouraging her. We had a great support system. Almost every time I went to the hospital, Liz would ask me to put my head on her belly so I could feel the babies. Then she asked me to talk to them. "They need to hear their father's voice," she would say. It was awkward at first because this was all new to me, but I got the hang of it. When I talked to them, I would greet them with, "Hey, guys. Hello, Mila. Hello, Mateo. This is Mondo." I didn't have the courage to say, "This is your dad." I always said, "This is Mondo." I was afraid to identify myself as a father. And Liz would kind of laugh, but then she would look at me and say, "It's OK to say dad."

When Liz went into labor, I was by her side for all thirty-one hours and twenty-six minutes. Our little girl, Mila, was the first to be delivered, and she was perfectly healthy. The instant I saw her, I fell in love. She was the most beautiful thing I'd ever seen in my life. Something shifted inside of me; a courage rose up. "Mila," I told her, "this is your dad. I love you. And I'm here to guide you. I'm here to protect you. I'm here to just be your father."

Almost immediately after Mila's birth, Liz had to start the laboring process all over again. After forty-six more minutes, Mateo was born. But when he came out, he was not breathing on his own. His body was gray. He wasn't responding the way Mila responded when she was born. I got so scared. I've never prayed so hard in my life as I did in that moment. The nurses began hustling around with intense purpose, working to resuscitate my son. I got next to Mateo, and I began to speak to him in Spanish. I said, "Mateo, this is Daddy. Mateo, this is your father. I'm your dad. Mateo, I love you. We've been expecting you, my son. I need to know that you're OK. Mateo, let me know that you're OK. Mateo, I need you to breathe, my son. I need you to fight. Mateo, I need you to breathe. Mateo, God loves you. I love you, Mateo. Your mom loves you. This is your dad. I love you, son. Let me know you're OK."

As I was speaking to him and praying over him, all of a sudden, I saw him lift his little thumb, as if to let me know he was OK. As I was watching this, I saw his body go from blue and gray to red, like the blood was flowing into him from the bottom of his feet all the way to the top of his head. And then he cried, and it was the most wonderful sound I'd ever heard in my life. In the past, when a baby cried, it made me anxious and fearful. This cry was different. This cry gave me life. This cry told me Mateo was OK. A joy burst from my inner being.

I recorded and have footage of all this, and we watch it every year on their birthday. Since that moment, I have always been involved in the twins' lives, twenty-four hours a day, seven days a week. When they were newborns, my wife would be up in the middle of the night feeding one baby, and I would be holding the other. We were—and are—a team.

Today, Liz, Mila, and Mateo are the greatest loves of my life. Mila and Mateo are two of the most beautiful people I've ever met. But more than that, they are two of the kindest, most polite and loving kids I've ever been around. Sometimes around the house, I have to go check on them because the house is so peaceful. They are thirteen years old now, and yet they still hug and kiss us and say, "Dad, I love you. Mom, I love you." Liz and I can be sitting in the kitchen, and they'll come by and just say, "I love you, Dad. I love you, Mom."

I never thought two of the greatest loves of my life would be two little kids. But they have taught me how to love. They are teaching me to be patient and kind. They have taught me that it's OK to be wrong, that it's OK to make mistakes, that I don't have to be perfect and have it all together. They are teaching me each day how to be a father. And loving them has helped me better understand the love God has for us. It's unconditional, a love that doesn't keep a record of wrongs. No matter what we look like, He responds with love.

Mila and Mateo are the greatest things in the world to me. My son and daughter tell me how proud they are of me. They remind me every single day that they love me. They often tell me how thankful they are that God chose them to be mine. My kids are the greatest gifts God could have ever given to me. My wife and I are so proud. We are so thankful that heaven gifted us with two angels named Mila and Mateo. God bringing them into my existence to make me better and teach me to love better is part of my crazy life.

Chapter 22

The Moments That Brought a Gangster to Grace

I HAVE NO DOUBT there was a bullet with my name on it waiting around the next corner, at the next phone booth, or in a back alley somewhere. But there was something bigger at work.

Who was there all the time, leading, protecting, and guiding me? Who was quietly shaping my destiny in the wilderness of life, though I remained unaware of the plan?

Think about it. We had been protected and provided for as we escaped the terrors of my father and civil war in Central America. Who sent people across our paths at the right times who allowed us to stay in their homes while we were in hiding? Why would my mom receive a prophetic word at church that we were being protected? And why would she receive the same exact word from a complete stranger at the resort? Why did we get such unusual favor from the US government at a critical time, declaring us full US citizens?

What kept me alive again and again in the streets of LA? What made Big Red from the Bloods show me unusual favor? What made the rival gangster on the bus show me unusual kindness by escorting me to my home neighborhood? What kept me from the phone booth, where I would have been gunned down?

Why did my sister get a passion to fast and pray for me? Then she received a prophetic word that I would be saved. How did she find the courage to step into my world and ask me the three questions that I could not get out of my mind— three questions that became a catalyst for me to find a way out of gang life and find hope.

Why did I feel something rising up inside me to get out of the car and walk away, even when a homie put a pistol in my face and threatened to blow me away? What was different about that church that night that made me feel peace and unconditional love? While those in the lowrider met the law and all went to prison, why did my mom make the connection with the Dream Center, where the Barnetts showed me unusual favor?

Why did I recover the stolen purse for a rival gang leader's mom, which led her sons to stop harassing me? How in the world did I end up meeting Jim Bakker, who became a father figure and mentor to me and trained me for a ministry in television, fulfilling the desire I'd had since I was a kid? Could there have been someone working on my behalf?

I had said repeatedly that I would never get married. But I ended up marrying a Lennon Sisters daughter in Branson, Missouri, of all places, years after that unusual moment when

I heard the Lennon Sisters in the holding cell. Where did the power to forgive my dad and those who murdered him come from? How did I come to accept the amazing gift of being a father—after saying for years that I didn't want kids—when my wife gave birth to healthy twins despite having a difficult pregnancy and labor?

You can't make up a scenario like this. The pieces of my life came together to make an original work of art, not a copy. God created the unique mosaic painting that has become my life.

I had no plans for these things to happen to me. Yet God knew what His plans were for me. Feelings of abandonment, rejection, loneliness, and brokenness left me thinking I was a mistake in this world. I thought everyone was out to hurt and use me. But when I read these words in the Bible for the first time, I cried: "'For I know the plans I have for you,' declares the Lord, 'plans to prosper you and not to harm you, plans to give you hope and a future'" (Jer. 29:11).

Even before I knew what my plans were, I was told by my own gang and society not to make any plans past eighteen years old because I was going to end up in prison, paralyzed in a wheelchair, or buried six feet underground. Meanwhile, God was working out His plans to lead me to the future He had for me. Knowing that changed everything for me.

You see, through Christ I found the ability to forgive those who had hurt me. I had been carrying the weight of resentment and bitterness. Unknowingly many people are living this way. Forgiveness is so powerful because when you choose to forgive, it gives you mental and emotional stability and you can start breaking the cycle of negative emotions—the anger, hurt, and constant replay of painful experiences.

Holding on to grudges impacted my overall well-being,

affecting my mental health, relationships, and personal growth. I learned through God's Word that I had been forgiven through Christ Jesus and that I was called to forgive others. Little did I know, that would take time. I had to be patient with myself. I had to process the impact of the trauma I experienced as a child so I could truly forgive from my heart. As I healed and matured in the areas where I had experienced pain, I was ready to forgive those who had hurt me.

But the hardest part was to accept that I had been forgiven for my actions. Learning that it was OK to forgive myself was life-changing for me; I got a taste of what it meant to be free. The more transparent I have become about my pain, brokenness, faults, and struggles, the stronger I have become. I surrendered to the fact that God loved me the way I was, but the good news is He refused to leave me that way. He wanted to make things right in my life.

What changed my life isn't a religion; it was having a personal relationship with Jesus. That enabled me to grow in the safety of His unconditional love. The same way I was forgiven, Christ wants to forgive you. I was living in torment because of sin, a condition that requires forgiveness and redemption. God doesn't want you to live in sin, a place of distress, anxiety, and uncertainty. He wants you to live and not just survive. The beauty about being free from shame, guilt, and hurt from the past is that it allows you to experience the abundant life He wants you to have (John 10:10).

No matter where you find yourself in life, no matter what you've done, regardless of your religious background or political affiliation, the same God who was with me on this crazy journey has a plan for you too. There is hope. No one is too far gone, too hopeless, or too sinful for God's grace. I am living proof. For me the hope started with my sister's questions: What if God is real? What if prayer works? What if I had a different destiny? Through all the pain and setbacks of my life God was in control, guiding the process. I ended up finding true love and acceptance, unlike anything the gang could ever give me.

With time I have learned to forgive from my heart and have allowed God to heal my wounded emotions. I found peace of mind and a purpose for my life. I was gifted with my wonderful wife, Liz, and our two kids, Mila and Mateo; my extended family; a ministry; and the ability to realize my passion and call to share my story around the world through the medium of television.

That's what God has done for me. He restores and makes us whole again. God brought me through all those trials so I could fulfill His call to bring the message of Christ's unconditional love to the world. Jesus wanted to live in my heart; He wanted me to have a heart like His—a pure, gentle heart, one not driven by vengeance. Instead, He wanted me to have a thankful heart, a heart full of joy, kindness, and love for humanity.

Nowadays, when I come across individuals who are in pain, lonely, shattered, and feeling rejected, I understand that I need to love them because we are all struggling with something. My goal is to build a relationship with them, to be part of their lives and tell them that they are loved, that they are not alone. Because of what I've been through, I am reminded to never stop loving hurting people. I don't believe in giving up on people so easily. We all develop differently. I still believe the church is a hospital for wounded and hurting people. But I am not ignorant to the fact that church leaders have too often set impossible standards and abused their parishioners spiritually and physically, hurting a lot of innocent people.

We all have shameful moments we don't want people to know about. Jesus knows full well that none of us is perfect. My spirit and soul were troubled when I was living in sin, longing for hope. Jesus said, "It is not the healthy people who need a doctor, but the sick. I did not come to invite good people but to invite sinners" (Mark 2:17, NCV).

Christ brought the good news of the gospel, and it is for whosoever will—that's you and me. The way I saw it, I had to get back to the cross, back to God, who gave us His one and only Son so that whoever believes in Him may not be lost but have eternal life. Christ came for the broken, the sick, the ones society deemed no good—people just like me.

I was tired; the heaviness of my life was weighing me down. I was in need of hope, and I received it! To this day the most gangster move I ever made was to give my life to Jesus Christ. That's me, and this is my crazy life!

Acknowledgments

WANT TO EXTEND a very special thanks to:

My father—I think of you every day of my life. Often in my dreams we meet and we sit, have coffee together, and talk about *fútbol* and how beautiful my life has become with my wife, Liz, and our twins, Mila and Mateo. Dad, despite our having a difficult time reconnecting and the pain of the past, when I think about how when I was little you were my hero, I want to tell you that today, as I age, you are in many ways still my hero. *Te amo, Papá.* (I love you, Dad.)

My mother—Mom, you are so special to me. Thank you for the sacrifice you made to provide and take care of us. I admire you for your courage and will to make it with two kids as a single mother, against all the odds. You were fearless, and you never gave up. Thank you for your unconditional love and for loving me through the hard moments we had together. Today, I am so thankful for you. Words cannot express the love I have for you, *madrecita linda.*

My sister—Laura, I am so grateful that you never gave up on me. When society and people around me lost hope, you never did. Privately, you prayed for a miracle to take place in my life. The bond we share is special. Our lives became so complicated, yet you saw early on that one day I would be sharing my story around the world. Thank you for praying for me and never

175

giving up on me. Because of what you did, I am here sharing my story to the world that miracles do happen. I love you and your beautiful family.

Pastors Tommy and Matthew Barnett and the Dream Center—thank you for giving me a chance, an opportunity to find my way. You saw the potential in me that gave me the courage to believe in myself. The Dream Center and the two of you will always hold a special place in my life.

Gary Smalley—the friendship we had was very meaningful in my life. You mentored me in so many ways. I could not understand why a world-renowned relationship counselor wanted to be a friend to this ex-gang member, but you did. You walked in at a time when I needed a friend. You have a special place in my heart. Thank you for officiating my wedding and your advice on relationships. But what impacted my life the most is how you helped my wife and me with groceries, diapers, wipes, and gifts when we were new parents of twins. I will never forget what you and Mama Norma did for us. My wife, our twins, and I love you so much, Gramps!

Jim Bakker—you have been very good to me, even when I didn't deserve it. Most of the people who have attacked, misunderstood, or vilified you did so because they didn't know you. They just read or saw the headlines about you. I never saw you fight back to defend yourself; you humbled yourself and kept your composure in public. I have gotten to know you very well. I saw firsthand the tears, the brokenness, and the pain it caused you, but you kept moving forward. You are a good man, sir. You are a man of your word; you walk in integrity. I've learned a lot of good from you. I will never be able to thank you enough for all you have done for me. You are my best friend, and I thank you for being a father I never had. I love you, man!

Lori Bakker—you are my second mom. Over the years you shared advice and wisdom that guided and taught me so much. Thank you for opening your home to me and always including me as part of the Bakker family. You calling me your son healed much pain and gave me a place to call home. You believed in me and gave me room to make mistakes but never gave up on me. I love you very much.

Grandma Char—your love was the cornerstone of the family and ministry, and I am deeply grateful for the warmth and wisdom you brought to our lives. Your unconditional love and resilience were a constant source of inspiration. Thank you for being the heart of our family and for the cherished memories we created together. I will always carry you in my heart.

Maricela, Lori, Clarissa, Marie, and Ricky—you will never know what you did for me. You gave me a freshness of life when I met you all. Thank you for trusting me in your lives, and know that I am so proud of each of you. My brother and sisters, you all prove that you don't have to be blood to be family. I love you.

John and Joyce Caruso—you will always hold a special place in my heart. Your love and kindness are unmatched. The advice you have given me throughout the last two decades has been invaluable. Thank you for loving and believing in me. My wife, my kids, and I love you both very much.

Ministry partners—thank you for your tireless dedication, your heartfelt contributions, and the profound impact you've made. Our collaboration is not just a partnership; it's a shared journey of purpose and meaning. I am honored to stand alongside each of you, and I look forward to continuing this incredible work together. Thank you for believing in me and welcoming me to the family.

Friends—to my old friends, thank you for the enduring memories and shared history. To my new friends, thank you for infusing my life with fresh perspectives and laughter. Your collective presence has made me a better person, and I am genuinely blessed to have such an incredible group of individuals as my friends. Thank you to each of you.

Extended family—to my aunts, uncles, and cousins: you've been more than family; you've been pillars of strength during times of need, sources of boundless love, and creators of unforgettable moments. Your love has transformed challenges into shared triumphs, and your unwavering support has been a comforting embrace. Thank you for being there when we needed you most and for filling our lives with the warmth of your love, the music of your laughter, and the lasting impressions of countless memories. With a heart full of gratitude and love, thank you.

Dr. Don and Mary Colbert—the two of you have meant so much to me. Spending time having breakfast that morning led to an incredible opportunity that I wasn't expecting. Your contribution to making this book happen is why I am able to share my story of finding hope. Thank you for believing in me.

Rick Renner—thank you for your friendship and for being so kind to me and my wife. The way you teach from Hebrew and the original Greek has given me a deeper understanding of Scripture and increased my love for the Bible.

R. T. Kendall—your message of forgiveness brought me to a place of stability in my life. The theological and fishing discussions we have shared throughout the years have changed my life. Thank you for your friendship.

Rick Joyner—you saw great potential in me when I was starting in ministry. You provided a vehicle and gave me a scholarship to be a part of your school and learn about Bible prophecy. But to be personally invited to sit at the prestigious roundtable is truly an honor for me. Thank you for believing in me.

Max Davis—thank you for joining me on this adventure to write this book. When we started, I was nervous and scared. Thank you for helping me capture the message behind the story and humanize a gang member. But most importantly, thank you for helping me put the past behind me.

Darryl Strawberry—you were the first one to call me to congratulate me on my book deal, and you reminded me that the streets had ideas of how we were going to end up but God had another plan for you and me. To call you a friend is still so surreal to me because you are a baseball legend. But more importantly, when we talk, you encourage me to stay close to Jesus, pray daily, love my wife, and stay present in my kids' lives. Thank you for your friendship. I love you and your wife, Tracy.

Mimi and Danny—thank you for welcoming me into your family. The love you have shown me has been so beautiful to experience. I have so much to be thankful for. The two of you have been there for everything—assisting us during the pregnancy and loving our babies, Mila and Mateo, these last thirteen years. I will forever be grateful. I love you both. You're the best in-laws in the world.

James and Mary—what the two of you mean to me is hard to describe in words because I have so much love for you and your kids. Thank you for the friendship and for never judging me for my past. You have made me feel welcomed in every way. I am so grateful to be part of your family, and it will always be special that your kids call me Uncle Vato.

The Lennon and Macias families—the love I received the moment I was introduced to you has helped me heal in areas where I had lost hope. Thank you for the unconditional love each of you has given me. I love you all.

Jason Rico—thank you for being the brother I never had. Your friendship helped me through difficult moments, and I'll never forget all the great moments I spent working with you, laughing all the time. I am so proud of you and the beautiful family you have. I know I can count on you anytime. Thank you for your friendship.

Mario Gonzalez—*¡Mi hermano!* Thank you for believing in me and always encouraging me to be better. I am grateful that we have stayed connected throughout the years. I am so proud of you. I know I can always count on you. Thank you for your friendship.

Raider Nation—anyone who knows me knows the Raiders have been my team since I discovered football as a kid. The Raiders had swag, confidence, toughness, passion, and a lot of heart to win. That has represented me. Years later, I am still rocking the Raiders hat, jacket, and the attitude to win. Thank you, Raider Nation, for inspiring kids like me to just win, baby!

Los Angeles Lakers—you gave me some of the best memories growing up watching Magic Johnson, Shaquille O'Neal, and the late Kobe Byrant. The purple and gold is LA. Thank you for giving us a way to forget about our troubles as we not only watched basketball but witnessed the Showtime Lakers in action.

Leo Messi and the Argentina national team—since I can remember I have been passionate about *fútbol*. I want to thank the Argentina national team for giving me a childhood filled with the hopes and dreams only a *fútbol* fan can understand. I will forever be grateful for the1986 FIFA World Cup championship, when Diego Armando Maradona scored two history-making goals. But watching Lionel Messi, arguably the best soccer player in the world, win the 2022 FIFA World Cup with my son, daughter, and wife by my side was a sports moment I will never forget. It brought so many tears as I remembered the times I spent with my dad back in 1986, watching Argentina in the World Cup. Thank you, Lionel Messi and the Argentina national team.

Finally, I humbly acknowledge and express gratitude to my Lord and Savior Jesus Christ, the embodiment of love, compassion, and grace. In moments of darkness His light has been a source of strength, guiding me toward hope and redemption. I am thankful for the profound impact of His love on my life. Lord, I am a sinner saved by grace, just an ex-gangster who fell in love with You, and I am so thankful that You saw beyond my faults.

Notes

PROLOGUE

1. Isaac Watts and R. E. Hudson, "En la Cruz," Hymnary.org, accessed November 3, 2023, https://hymnary.org/text/herido_triste_a_jesus.
2. Isaac Watts and Ralph E. Hudson, "At the Cross," Hymnary.org, accessed November 3, 2023, https://hymnary.org/hymn/BH2008/255.

CHAPTER 14

1. Watts and Hudson, "En la Cruz"; Watts and Hudson, "At the Cross."

About the Author

Mondo De La Vega is a motivational speaker who shares his life story and the lessons he has learned along the way. Fluent in English and Spanish, he speaks at churches, conferences, and events throughout the world.

Contact him at mondodelavega@gmail.com to speak at your next event.

Or visit the following websites for more information:

www.mondodelavega.com

www.themondoshow.com

Mondo's national television program, *The Mondo Show*, airs Mondays and Wednesdays at 7 p.m. on The PTL Network, and is available on demand at ptlnetwork.com/the-mondo-show/.

You can also view *The Mondo Show* by downloading the official PTL Network app FREE to any smartphone, Roku, Apple TV, or Amazon Fire TV Stick.